Smart Ways

to Save Money

During & After

DIVORCE

by Victoria F. Collins, Ph.D., CFP & Ginita Wall, CPA, CFP

NOLO PRESS ⚖ BERKELEY

YOUR RESPONSIBILITY WHEN USING A SELF-HELP LAW BOOK

We've done our best to give you useful and accurate information in this book. But this book does not take the place of a lawyer licensed to practice law in your state. If you want legal advice, see a lawyer. If you use any information contained in this book, it's your personal responsibility to make sure that the facts and general information contained in it are applicable to your situation.

KEEPING UP-TO-DATE

To keep its books up-to-date, Nolo Press issues new printings and new editions periodically. New printings reflect minor legal changes and technical corrections. New editions contain major legal changes, major text additions or major reorganizations. To find out if a later printing or edition of any Nolo book is available, call Nolo Press (510-549-1976) or check the catalog in the *Nolo News*, our quarterly newspaper.

To stay current, follow the "Update" service in the Nolo News. You can get the paper free by sending us the registration card in the back of the book. In another effort to help you use Nolo's latest materials, we offer a 25% discount off the purchase of any new Nolo book if you turn in any earlier printing or edition. (See the "Recycle Offer" in the back of the book.) This book was last printed in June 1994.

FIRST EDITION	June 1994
EDITOR	Robin Leonard
BOOK DESIGN	Jackie Mancuso
PRODUCTION	Michelle Duval
PROOFREADER	Anne Hayes
INDEX	Mary Kidd
PRINTING	Delta Lithograph

COPYRIGHT © 1994 BY VICTORIA F. COLLINS AND GINITA WALL

PRINTED IN THE UNITED STATES OF AMERICA

ALL RIGHTS RESERVED

Felton-Collins, Victoria.
    Smart ways to save money before and after divorce / by Victoria Felton-Collins & Ginita Wall. —1st national ed.
    p.   cm.
    Includes index.
    ISBN 0-87337-214-X :
    1. Divorce—Law and legislation—United States—Popular works. 2. Divorce—United States—Costs—Popular works. 3. Divorce settlements—United States—Popular works. 4. Divorce—Economic aspects—United States—Popular works.   I. Wall, Ginita.
    II. Title.
    K535.Z9F45   1994
    346.7301'66—dc20
    [347.306166]   94-353
                               CIP

DEDICATION

We dedicate this book to everyone experiencing divorce—

Those going through it know it's not easy. There *is* life after divorce and we wish you the very best as you move toward it.

Those who provide guidance (attorneys, mediators, financial advisers, therapists) know it's not simple.

We hope this book will help make it less costly in every way.

ACKNOWLEDGMENTS

No book is ever the result of the authors' efforts alone. The many clients, attorneys, financial professionals and therapists who have shared information and insights over the years (and yes, horror stories as well) have helped form the theme for this book. We called on the expertise of our professional colleagues attorney/mediator Alicia Taylor, who provided insight into the mediation process, attorney and certified family law specialist Michele Sacks Lowenstein, who helped research issues and was a valued sounding board, attorney Alexander C. Verduci, who provided expert guidance on military issues, and tax attorney Jerry Hesch, who helped brainstorm creative tax-saving ideas. We found these experts not only willing to share ideas, but wonderfully supportive in every respect. Thanks also go to attorney Violet Woodhouse, with whom Victoria co-authored *Divorce and Money*, for her unflagging concern over the contents of this book.

Special thanks go to the team at Nolo (especially Jake Warner and Steve Elias for reading and critiquing the manuscript) and to our outstanding editor Robin Leonard. Robin has been both a friend and an inspiration. Her astute input, challenging questions, legal expertise, wonderful support (and comments that were even readable) all went toward making this book the best it could be.

CONTENTS

PART 1

KEEPING ATTORNEYS' FEES LOW

PART 2

SAVING ON ALIMONY

PART 3

PAYING AND RECEIVING CHILD SUPPORT PAINLESSLY

PART 4

SAVING TAX DOLLARS

PART 5

UNDERSTANDING THE TAX CONSEQUENCES OF THE HOUSE

PART 6

GETTING YOUR FAIR SHARE OF ASSETS

       Frequent Flyer Points
       Vacation and Sick Pay
       Season Tickets
       Club Memberships
       Stock Options
       Timeshares
       Magazine Subscriptions and Professional Dues
       Prepaid Insurance

PART 7

TAKING ACTION NOW FOR BENEFITS LATER

PART 8

SAVING MONEY AFTER THE DIVORCE

APPENDIX A—SOURCES OF TAXABLE INCOME

APPENDIX B—SOURCES OF NON-TAXABLE INCOME

PART I

KEEPING ATTORNEYS' FEES LOW

You have come to the realization that your marriage is not working and you are considering a divorce. This may not be an easy time—divorce is one of the most stressful events a person can endure. But you don't have to add to your anxiety by worrying excessively about money.

You have no doubt heard about attorneys' fees and the high cost of divorce. In this section, however, you will learn how to keep the cost of divorce low. First, you'll see how critical it is to separate emotions from economics in the divorce process. Second, you'll decide exactly what professionals you need to work with. You may conclude that you don't need to hire an attorney or that you can consult with one just to answer a few questions. Another way to save money is to use a mediator to help you resolve disputed issues. And if you need more financial advice than legal advice, you may conclude that your best help will come from an accountant, appraiser or other financial advisor, not a lawyer. If you do work with an attorney, you'll learn several tips that will save you money, such as keeping a telephone log, reaching a fee and services agreement and taking a very active role in your divorce.

CONSIDER DOING YOUR DIVORCE WITHOUT AN ATTORNEY

Do you need an attorney, or can you handle your divorce yourself? (Representing yourself in your divorce—that is, not hiring a lawyer—is called handling your case *pro se* or *pro per*.) Even if you can handle the divorce alone, should you? You may be wrestling with these questions right now. Before you expend too much time, energy or money, let's look at some guidelines to help you decide.

Answer the following questions true or false:

T   F

☐   ☐   1. You and your spouse have simply grown apart. You are both interested in getting a divorce and feel relatively amicable toward each other.

☐   ☐   2. You've always shared the family finances openly and have each kept the other informed about spending, saving, investing, taxes, retirement plans and property you own.

☐   ☐   3. You have been married for no more than five years and both of you are working or capable of supporting yourselves.

❏ ❏   4. If you have minor children, you and your spouse generally agree on values in child rearing.

❏ ❏   5. You truly believe your spouse is a good and capable parent and that together you can reach agreements about custody, visitation and child support that will be fair to both and in your children's best interest.

❏ ❏   6. Your marriage has been punctuated by affairs, abuse and/or extreme conflict.

❏ ❏   7. One spouse is on active military duty or is a retired military professional.

❏ ❏   8. Your spouse has managed the family finances and you have little or no information, or you have controlled the family finances and your spouse has little or no information.

❏ ❏   9. Your spouse has a large (or several) pensions, all or most of which were earned during the marriage.

❏ ❏ 10. You and your spouse have accumulated a lot of property together, and you aren't particularly sophisticated about finances.

If you answered true to all or most of the first five and false to all or most of the last five questions, chances are good that you may be able to handle your divorce yourself. If however, your answers to the first five included two or three falses and a true to two or more of the last five, you'll most likely need the services of an attorney.

Here's another way to consider it. If your finances are complex and include military pensions and benefits, or a family-owned business or marital property hard to value or hard to divide, you'll need the services of a competent attorney and/or an accountant, actuary, appraiser or other financial professional. If your marriage includes a history of dishonesty, abuse or a power imbalance, using an attorney will be essential.

On the other hand, if you and your spouse have a fairly equal division of financial knowledge and a true commitment to getting through this with the least amount of damage, you should consider doing your own divorce. A recent study indicated that *pro per* and *pro se* (without an attorney) divorces tend to occur in:

- short marriages
- with young people
- who have more debts than assets
- who have little or no property
- who have no children or clearly agree who will have custody.[1]

In a surprising number of *pro se* divorces, the defendant (the person against whom the divorce is filed) is out of the picture—left town, joined the military or moved in with someone else.

Indeed, the fastest growing part of the divorce preparation business is non-lawyer divorce typing services (independent paralegals) who help people complete their own divorce papers. For about $175–$250, these services prepare *all* divorce paperwork under the supervision of customers, who typically get the necessary information from a self-help law book. On the west coast and in Arizona, Texas, Florida and some other states, these businesses are easy to find (check "divorce assistance" or "lawyer alternatives" in your phone book or the business section in your newspaper's classifieds).

As with all professional services, there are ranges of competence. You will want to ask the same questions about qualifications, experience, services and fees that you would when you engage the help of any professional.

There are three main reasons why you will want to give serious consideration to doing your own divorce.

To Save Money. Using an attorney will cost a minimum of $1,500 to $5,000 per spouse for uncomplicated cases and most likely will be significantly higher than that. Statistics show that the average cost of a divorce when lawyers are used to resolve issues in large urban areas such as Los

---

[1]*Self-Representation in Divorce Cases,* The American Bar Association Standing Committee on the Delivery of Legal Services. Copies are available from the ABA, 750 N. Lake Shore Dr., Chicago, IL 60611

Angeles is about $18,000 per spouse. One matrimonial lawyer stated in early 1994 that each spouse would have to pay a lawyer $5,000 to obtain an *uncontested* divorce in New York City. (Warning! Lawyers who advertise on TV about low rates are almost always misleading. Their fees are for uncontested divorces without having to make a court appearance or do much background research. If they have to go to court to gather financial information, their fees will rise dramatically.)

To Achieve a Better Outcome. From what we've seen in our practices, people who take an active role in negotiating their divorce settlements reach better settlements than do those people who leave the negotiating to their lawyers. What we mean by "better" is less post-divorce conflict and litigation, better compliance with agreements, more good will between ex-spouses and better sharing of information about children and parenting in general.

To Minimize Emotional Damage and Maximize Personal Recovery. The adversarial system operates on the assumption that only by fighting will the "truth" emerge. Although this is a false assumption, many divorcing spouses buy into it, and hire lawyers to "win" their case. When this happens, a simple case—even one with certain basic understandings already reached and a degree of good will between the spouses—can quickly turn into a complex case full of suspicion, mistrust, emotional damage and big lawyer's bills. As many can attest, recovering emotionally from a nasty and expensive divorce is neither easy nor fun. Doing it yourself can speed the emotional recovery because your mind is focused on practical things, you are encouraged to interact with your spouse in a sensitive and compassionate manner (or at least in a non-combative manner) and you have a sense of control which helps overcome the helpless feeling many people have.

If you do decide to do your divorce without a lawyer, you will be far from alone. In California, Arizona and several other states, more than 60% of filers handle their own divorces. In 50% of the divorces filed in Florida, at least one spouse is representing himself or herself.

While the answer to "can you handle your own divorce?" may be yes, the answer to "should you?" may turn out to be no. In the process of doing it yourself, if any of the following occurs, you may need to seek the help of an attorney—for a short consultation or for representation:

- Hostility becomes so intense you are unable to discuss your settlement or divorce rationally. (Often this means a lawyer, but not always. If you have no children and no or little property, you can probably still do your own divorce even if you hate each other.)
- You feel confused about your rights or overwhelmed by the financial and/or legal complexities. (If you are only feeling confused or overwhelmed by your finances, however, consider using the services of an accountant, actuary, appraiser or other financial professional as appropriate. This may provide the clarification you need.)
- Your spouse files legal papers that are in contradiction to or outside of the context of your discussions and agreements.

If you decide to use an attorney, bear in mind that there are ways to keep fees low and we cover them throughout this section. Legal aid society, legal services, legal clinics, or law schools in your area may also provide competent low cost legal aid or be able to make referrals to meet your needs.

Help for Self-Helpers

- *Divorce: A New Yorker's Guide to Doing It Yourself,* by Bliss Alexandra (Nolo Press). This book contains all the forms and instructions for doing your divorce in the Empire State without a lawyer.
- *How to Do Your Own Divorce,* by Charles Sherman (Nolo Occidental) California and Texas Editions. The book that launched Nolo Press and

the self-help law movement in the early 1970s contains the forms and instructions for doing your divorce without a lawyer. Available for Californians and Texans.

• *Divorce and Money: How to Make the Best Financial Decisions During Divorce,* by Violet Woodhouse and Victoria F. Collins, with M.C. Blakeman (Nolo Press). This book contains practical advice and step-by-step guidance on dividing property, settling child support and alimony, and maintaining your sanity during divorce.

NO-FAULT DIVORCE

No-fault divorce describes any divorce in which the spouse suing for divorce does not have to accuse the other of wrongdoing. Rather, the spouse can simply state that the couple no longer is compatible, or that the couple has been living apart for a specified period.

Until the 1970s, the only way a person could get a divorce was to prove that the other spouse was guilty of marital misconduct (such as mental cruelty, abandonment or adultery) and was at fault for the marriage not working. Today, all states allow divorces regardless of who is "at fault."

No-fault divorces are usually granted for reasons such as incompatibility, irreconcilable differences, or irretrievable or irremediable breakdown of the marriage.

Incompatibility refers to a conflict in personalities that makes married life together impossible.

Irreconcilable differences are differences that are considered sufficiently severe to make married life together more or less impossible. As a practical matter, courts seldom, if ever, inquire into what the differences actually are, and routinely grant a divorce as long as the party seeking the divorce says the couple has irreconcilable differences.

Irremediable or irretrievable breakdown in a marriage occurs when one spouse refuses to live with the other and will not work toward reconciliation. As a practical matter, courts seldom, if ever, inquire into whether the marriage has actually broken down, and routinely grant a divorce as long as the party seeking the divorce says it has.

- *Divorce Yourself: The National No-Fault Divorce Kit*, by Daniel Sitarz (Nova Press). This book contains general information and generic forms for obtaining a no-fault divorce. It cannot be used in states with mandatory divorce court forms; however, it can provide you with an introduction to no-fault divorce if *nothing* else is available in your state. Be sure to exhaust all avenues for a guide specific to your state before relying on this book.
- *California Divorce Help Line* (800-359-7004). Lawyers and paralegals provide legal help to California residents at $10 per call and $2.50 per minute; most calls last fewer than 15 minutes.
- *TeleLawyer* (800-283-5529). Available for people in all states; TeleLawyer charges by the minute for legal information and advice.
- Check your local law library, public library or bookstore for a state-specific book on doing your own divorce. These books come and go with great frequency, so be sure the book you use is the most current edition. Some of these books are quite good; others are not. Spend a bit of time studying your choices. Look for books that give helpful, current and complete information. Avoid books that tell you to go see a lawyer on every other page.

JUDGING A GOOD SELF-HELP LAW BOOK

More and more consumers are using self-help books and software to handle all kinds of legal tasks, including divorce. But the quality of self-help law products, like that of lawyers, varies widely. To tell a good self-help law product from a bad one, ask the following questions before buying:

1. Can you get your money back? Some people find, after buying a self-help law product, that they are in over their heads. Other people find that the

product did not live up to its promise of providing "all forms and instructions" to help you file for divorce. If you want your money back, you should be able to get it back, no questions asked.

2. Is the product up-to-date? Never use out-of-date legal materials. Laws change, and your efforts will be wasted if you use obsolete forms or rely on a law that is no longer in force. As a general rule, any product that has not been updated within the last two years is suspect.

3. Does the product give you enough information? Every task that can be defined as legal involves a number of choices. These choices can profoundly affect your income, property and personal relationships. If you are going to fill out forms or draft documents (such as a settlement agreement), you need enough background information to know what you are doing and why.

4. Is the product written for your state? Divorce varies tremendously from one state to the next. Even the language used to describe divorce isn't the same throughout our country. For example, alimony is called spousal support in California and maintenance in New York. A national book cannot address all the specific divorce laws of your state.

5. Are all procedures explained step-by-step? A good self-help product should tell you how to fill out every blank of every form or provide sample documents you can adapt to your needs. And it should help you face the complex and often confusing requirements of courts. What forms do you use? How many copies do you need? Is there a filing fee? Where can you get more information?

6. Can you understand the documents you are signing? A good self-help law product provides documents in which every clause is either written in plain English or clearly explained. You should understand what you are signing.

7. Does the product warn you when you are in over your head? No self-help law product, no matter how good, can handle every possible legal situation. A good product should cover a reasonable range of the most common situations and warn you when your situation is too unusual or complex to be handled without professional help.

CONSIDER USING A MEDIATOR

If you and your spouse don't agree on important issues, such as the division of property or child custody or support, it doesn't mean you still can't do your own divorce. Before turning the matter over to an expensive lawyer, you can try to resolve your disputes through mediation.

Mediators work with both spouses to help them resolve their own problems. Mediation is especially advantageous with couples who will have an ongoing relationship after the divorce, such as parents of minor children.

Mediators charge by the session, hour or day, and may be marriage and family counselors or attorneys. Those who are attorneys generally charge their standard fee ($125 an hour and up). Those who are therapists, psychologists, ministers or social workers usually have fees which are lower than attorneys' and some even have a sliding scale based on ability to pay.

The hourly fee is not the only area in which you will realize savings. Typically, mediation takes far less time than using lawyers takes to settle the issues. For example, five days of mediation at $150 an hour may cost $6,000 (full eight-hour days) while a two day trial with all the preliminaries—discovery, depositions, motions, pre-trial settlement conferences, court reporter and the rest—would probably cost $25,000 and produce the same or a worse result. Of course, you can combine the two—that is, settle your issues through mediation, but consult an attorney on your own between mediation sessions to help you clarify your position.

After mediation, use lawyers to review the agreement you reached with the mediator and to file the divorce papers and complete the divorce. Or you can do the paperwork on your own or with the help of a typing service.

What to Expect in Working With a Mediator

- You'll share costs equally with your spouse.
- You'll meet together with your spouse and the mediator.
- The mediator will be an impartial third party, who will assist you in reaching a solution that is a compromise for both, but will not take sides.
- The mediator will draft a memorandum of understanding which summarizes the agreements you reach.
- You will then use an attorney (or one for each of you), a typing service or yourself to draft the agreement in legal form. (A mediator-attorney will probably draft the agreement for you as part of the mediation process.)

How to Judge if Mediation Is Right for You

These questions will help you evaluate if mediation is appropriate for you. Don't just ask these questions when considering mediation; ask them throughout the mediation process, as your emotions, needs and goals will most likely change many times as you move forward.

- Can we each stand up for ourselves emotionally?
- Is one of us intimidated by the other? Has one been abused by the other?
- Are we both committed to what is fair?
- Does one of us feel forced to try mediation?
- Can we each express our thoughts clearly and can we hear the other?

- Do we feel willing to compromise and try for a "win-win" solution?
- Is financial knowledge and power pretty evenly balanced in our relationship?

ADDITIONAL MEDIATION TIPS

Gary J. Friedman, attorney and mediator, is the author of *A Guide to Divorce Mediation: How to Reach a Fair, Legal Settlement at a Fraction of the Cost* (Workman Publishing). He identifies four criteria indispensable for successful mediation:

- Motivation to mediate—Mediation will undoubtedly fail if one of you feels forced into it.
- Self-responsibility—You must understand your own situation and set your own priorities.
- Willingness to disagree—You must be able to stand up for yourself and refuse a settlement that won't let you move ahead with your life.
- Willingness to agree—Obviously, mediation can't work if you won't strive for an agreement.

A Guide to Divorce Mediation is a must if you are considering mediation as a way to handle the unresolved areas of your divorce. The book is available in libraries and bookstores.

How to Find a Mediator

- Ask friends and professionals whose judgment you trust for referrals.
- Contact your county family or domestic relations court for referrals. If your state requires or authorizes judges to order mediation to resolve child custody disputes, you may be able to get a referral from the court clerk to a private mediator to handle *any* aspect of your divorce—not just child custody. California, Delaware, Florida (circuits with family

mediation programs), Idaho, Maine, Maryland, Nevada (counties with mediation programs), New Mexico, North Carolina, Oregon and Utah (counties with pilot mediation programs) require mediation in custody and visitation disputes. Alaska, Colorado, Connecticut, Florida (circuits without family mediation program), Illinois, Iowa, Kansas, Louisiana, Massachusetts, Michigan, Minnesota, North Dakota, Rhode Island, Texas, Utah (counties without pilot mediation programs), Vermont, Washington and Wisconsin authorize judges to order mediation.

- Contact the American Academy of Family Mediators, 1500 South Highway 100, Suite 355, Golden Valley, MN 55416. The Academy provides a national referral service and can send you a list of practitioners in your state.
- Some judicial arbitration services (discussed below) offer mediation.
- Check the phone book under mediation as a last resort.

Arbitration

If you decide mediation is not for you, or you've begun mediation and don't want to continue, this does not mean your only choice is full-blown litigation.

Another option to consider is *arbitration*. Arbitration is useful when most issues have been decided and you are on your way to a final dissolution but are still "hung up" on some critical points such as the value of a business or the amount of alimony. (Some states may prohibit the arbitration of child support and/or child custody.)

Both parties go before an arbitrator (often a retired judge from the family court) and present their case with or without their own attorneys. The arbitrator then makes a decision regarding the disputed issues. The decision is incorporated into a court judgment and is just as valid as if a judge had decided the issues. As compared to a court battle, there is money to be saved in most cases by using a "rent a judge." This is especially true for upper income couples, who can afford the up-front payment for the services of an arbitrator, which can be as high as $350 per hour. You are not bogged down by the costly waiting for trial or other court procedures. The arbitrator is dedicated to your case until it is resolved.

Check the phone book under "arbitration" or with an attorney or your local bar association to find arbitration or "rent a judge" services. In California, for example, the best known service is JAMS (Judicated Arbitration and Mediation Services).

GET THE HELP YOU NEED

If your divorce is complicated, get the professional help you need.

If you or your spouse own a business, have hard-to-value assets, are already engaged in other legal proceedings, such as bankruptcy, or are disputing ownership of an item of valuable property (for instance, you say it's yours and your spouse says you own it jointly), you have a complicated divorce and may need the help of an attorney who has additional training in family law, and possibly an accountant or financial professional.

Even if your divorce is complex, you don't necessarily need to hire a lawyer to take the whole case. Often, one or both of you can buy advice by the hour, after getting as much information as possible through self-study (see list of resources in Smart Way number 1). This self-help law coach model is the big coming trend, probably to be endorsed by the American Bar Association and some state bar groups. By unbundling services, you buy the expertise you need, not the paper shuffling and lawyers' attitudes you don't need.

Don't assume that a long marriage or a lot of assets means your divorce is complicated. Certainly children alone do not complicate matters if the parents agree on custody and child support. And even if you agree on child custody but disagree on child support, all states now determine the amount by formula, leaving little room for argument. But remember—if you do your own divorce, accept the fact that you may need help from a professional such as an accountant, financial advisor, stock broker, realtor, banker and others. In short, get the help you need and use the help you get.

GET SPECIALIZED INFORMATION

There are several unusual situations that can make divorce more costly, more frustrating or more time-consuming than it already is. You will need specialized information, if any of the following are true for you:

- Your spouse is out of the state or country and is unwilling to cooperate in obtaining the divorce. In this case, you have three potential problems: serving papers on your spouse, discovering what assets exist and getting your share of those assets. You can divorce a missing spouse by filing for divorce and publishing notice of the filing in a local newspaper. A judge can grant you a divorce, even if your spouse does not respond to the published notice, and if your spouse has property within the state the court can generally make orders to satisfy your need for support from that property. Generally, assets can be divided no matter where located, but the court of your state will have limited control over your spouse or your spouse's assets if they are out of state.

- Your spouse is seriously mentally incapacitated. Divorce makes everyone a little crazy, it is true. But if your spouse is seriously mentally ill and unable to act on her own behalf, a court may need to appoint a guardian or conservator to represent her interests in a divorce case. If you suspect that your spouse is not capable of dealing competently for herself, consult an attorney before filing for divorce. If you don't, and negotiate a settlement with your spouse, that settlement could be set aside if a court later declares your spouse incompetent.

- Your spouse dies during divorce. Even though you may wish that he would, you may regret it if he does. If he dies before the divorce is final, the court no longer has the right to hear your case and settle the property division issues. Unless he left everything to you in his will or a trust, or your property automatically goes to you because you still have it in joint tenancy, you'll probably find yourself in the probate court, doing battle with his heirs.

- One of you is a non-resident alien. If you are a U.S. resident married to a non-resident alien, the state courts will have little control over your spouse for the purpose of awarding you property support from property located outside of the country. If you are married to a non-resident alien, any profit (gain) on property you transfer to your spouse in your divorce will be taxable to you.

- One of you is in bankruptcy (or is headed that way). Money troubles and marriage troubles go hand in hand. If you are having financial difficulty and might be headed for bankruptcy, read Smart Way number 64 carefully.

WRITE A SUMMARY OF IMPORTANT FACTS

Whether you are going it alone, using a mediator, using an attorney to help with only specific issues or hiring an attorney to handle the entire case, you'll want to prepare an outline of the important facts of your marriage. If you go it alone, you'll save time and aggravation by bringing this information together, and you can then focus on the tasks that need to be done. If you work with a professional, the better prepared and focused you are, the more time and money you'll save. Basically, all divorces require the following information:

- The date you married.
- Your children's birth dates.
- The dates that you and your spouse may have previously been separated—that is, lived apart with the intention of ending the marriage.
- A list of your property, plus the following about each item:

✓ approximate date acquired

✓ current market value

✓ debts against it (such as mortgage or liens)

✓ original cost, and

✓ tax basis of the item—for real property, this is what you paid plus any improvements minus any tax benefits received. For mutual funds, stocks or bonds, it is what you paid plus reinvested interest, dividends and capital gains. This information is important in determining your tax liability when you sell the item.

- The property either of you brought into the marriage or inherited or acquired by gift during marriage. (This is generally considered your separate property.)

- The monthly and periodic (such as quarterly) income for you and your spouse.

- The monthly and periodic (such as annual) expenses for you and your spouse.

By gathering this information and making a list of your property, you are taking the first step toward determining if you need a lawyer, can go it alone or need a mediator. If you can agree on what's yours, what's mine and how to divide what's ours, consider going it alone. If the list of items you disagree about is short, using a mediator will probably be the best way to go. If disagreements run throughout your list, you'll probably need a lawyer to get through your divorce.

Also, make a list of questions in preparation for meetings with your attorney or financial professional. This will save time and therefore *fees,* especially if the lawyer is "coaching" you through your divorce or otherwise helping you in a limited capacity.

Sample Questions for a Lawyer

- Other than the property I brought into the marriage and/or inherited or acquired by gift during the marriage (and didn't mix with my spouse's property or our jointly owned property), do I have any property which might be considered my separate property?
- Do our state laws allow me to withdraw half of the cash in our joint accounts?
- Can my spouse change the title (how the property is held, such as joint tenants or tenants in common) on our property without my consent?
- What portion of the fees paid to you are tax deductible?
- What portion of our retirement benefits is marital property and subject to division?

GATHER FINANCIAL RECORDS

Gather as much information and as many financial documents as possible. By doing this, you'll save time and money whether you are handling the divorce yourselves, settling issues with the help of a mediator, using a typing service to prepare your papers, consulting a lawyer for specialized help or hiring a lawyer to handle the entire case.

Paperwork should include information showing what you own and what you owe (sometimes called a net worth statement or balance sheet), and information showing your income and expenses. This information is important in reaching decisions about property division, alimony and child support. In addition, locate loan applications and documents, financial statements, brokerage statements, tax returns for five years for you and your businesses. It will also be helpful to have bank statements, canceled checks, check registers, real estate deeds and insurance policies.

Ask your spouse first for any information you might not have. In an uncontested divorce, where you just want to divorce and move on, your spouse will probably cooperate in giving you information.

If she is unwilling to provide it and you cannot locate the information from other sources, you may be able to obtain it directly from the original source. For example, you may obtain copies of your loan application and loan documents from the lending institution. Real estate deeds are on file at the county records office. Your insurance agent can give you copies of your policies. Copies of your bank statements are available directly from your bank for a nominal fee, though retrieving copies of each canceled check is usually prohibitively expensive. If you don't have copies of your personal income tax returns, you may obtain them by filing Form 4506 with the IRS and paying a small fee. You will also be able to obtain copies of business returns directly from the IRS if you signed the copy that was filed. Request that the copies of these forms be sent directly to you or to your attorney, a friend or your post office box.

Your spouse may suggest that you don't need the missing financial records and that she is willing to give you generous settlement terms. Remember, however, that you and your spouse now have separate, and to some extent competing, economic interests, so be skeptical of any seemingly generous offer. Perhaps your spouse *is* being fair or feeling so guilty she is going overboard to give you the lion's share of the marital property. But at least as often, your spouse is withholding some vital information or trying to smooth talk you into making concessions or giving away important rights.

This is more likely to occur if you are reasonably affluent and have a fair number of complicated assets. Before evaluating your spouse's offer, gather all your financial records and enlist the help of an accountant or financial planner to help you determine the "big picture" of where you stand financially.

Gathering financial information such as this will save you time with your attorney (and therefore fees) for consultation and legal information collecting (called discovery). It may also save you from accepting a seemingly generous offer that later turns out to cost you in terms of property division or support.

BE PROACTIVE

Take an active role in your divorce. If you use a mediator, stop the process if your spouse tries to take over, the mediator tries to impose answers on you or you don't feel the mediator is listening to you. If you are going it alone, don't let your spouse take over and don't assume she will operate with both of your best interests in mind. If you use an attorney, remember that this is your divorce, not your attorney's. Your attorney will give you advice, but the decisions should rest with you. If you and your spouse are able to communicate, negotiate as much of the divorce directly with your spouse as possible to save attorney fees.

Many child-related issues are best negotiated directly by the two of you, such as physical custody and specific dates and times of visitation. You and your spouse may also be able to reach general agreements on some or all property issues, such as who will live in the house, whether it will be sold, how retirement assets will be divided, whether the division will be now or at retirement, and so forth. You may want to use attorneys and/or a competent accountant to pin down the details regarding valuation, title and tax issues. Even if your attorney negotiates for you, formulate specific financial goals and understand the nuances of the financial issues so you obtain the best possible settlement.

Specific Recommendations for Being Active in Your Divorce

- Study a book on do-it-yourself divorce even if you plan to use an attorney. A state-specific divorce guide or a general self-help guide where no state-specific book exists will give you a good education about the legal process and the legal forms. That will enable you to be a more active participant in the divorce process and will save a great deal of time your attorney might otherwise have spent explaining legalities to you.
- If you enjoy technical classes, consider taking one in divorce procedures as part of a paralegal program at a local college or university. This will certainly help you if you plan to do the paperwork yourself. If you intend to get legal help, taking a class will help you better understand the process and the role of your attorney.
- Share general financial information on topics related to your divorce with your spouse. For example, send your spouse a copy of this book or *Divorce and Money,* as well as relevant articles from magazines such as *Money, Kiplinger's Personal Finance, Smart Money* or *Worth.*
- Set appointments with your spouse to discuss specific issues. Prepare an agenda ahead of time, meet in a neutral place (like a restaurant

neither of you have eaten in before) where memories and conflict are less likely to surface, set the length of the meeting and don't exceed it.

- Take a class in negotiation skills and/or dealing with difficult people. Chances are you'll both be difficult during this time!
- If there is something you don't understand or don't feel comfortable with, *ask* your spouse, the mediator or your attorney. Don't make assumptions or jump to conclusions.

Recommended Reading

- *Divorce and Money: How to Make the Best Financial Decisions During Divorce,* by Violet Woodhouse and Victoria F. Collins, with MC Blakeman (Nolo Press). Practical advice and step-by-step guidance on dividing property, settling child support and alimony, and maintaining your sanity during divorce.
- *Nolo's Pocket Guide to Family Law,* by Robin Leonard and Stephen Elias (Nolo Press).
- *Legal Research: How to Find and Understand the Law,* by Stephen Elias and Susan Levinkind (Nolo Press).
- *Divorce: A New Yorker's Guide to Doing It Yourself,* by Bliss Alexandra (Nolo Press). Contains all the forms and instructions for doing your divorce in the Empire State without a lawyer.
- *How to Do Your Own Divorce,* by Charles Sherman (Nolo Press) California and Texas Editions. Contains all the forms and instructions for doing your divorce without a lawyer.

- *Dancing With Lawyers—How to Take Charge and Get Results,* by Nicholas Carroll (Royal Baker Press).
- *A Guide to Divorce Mediation: How to Reach a Fair, Legal Settlement at a Fraction of the Cost,* by Gary J. Friedman (Workman Publishing).
- State Bar Associations pamphlets on divorce. You can find the phone number for your state bar by calling directory assistance in your state capital or other large city. Also the American Bar Association publishes *Your Legal Guide to Marriage and Other Relationships.* Send $2 to: Order Fulfillment, American Bar Association, 750 North Lake Shore Drive, Chicago, IL 60611.

SEPARATE EMOTIONS FROM ECONOMICS

Insist that your divorce not turn into an emotional battleground. While it may be tempting to use money as a weapon, or to be vindictive, that type of emotional behavior will lead to a contested divorce and only cost you more in the long run. The hardest part is managing your own emotions. In fact, it may be impossible to do this without help from a therapist or wise friend. The outcome of a legal action on most issues in divorce is highly predictable and you have a lot to lose from a contested lawsuit. The higher the emotions, the longer the proceedings and the more costly the divorce. If you can keep your own emotional issues separate from the legal and financial issues of your divorce, you can keep your divorce under control.

Divorce is a time of great sadness. Know that there will be times that your grief is overwhelming. Do your crying at home or at a friend's house, not in your attorney's office at $175 per hour or the mediator's office at $125 per hour.

Specific Recommendations

- Understand all the steps to the divorce process and think about your overall strategy. You don't have to solve all your problems immediately. It is no better or worse to take a short time or a long time in negotiating a divorce. The key is to avoid a contested divorce. Take your time, and adhere to your own rhythm and timetable.
- Be clear on your position on two or three big issues such as custody and support. Then be prepared to make concessions on the issues you care less about. This will result in a better settlement and probably lower legal fees.
- Insist that all contested issues be mediated or arbitrated. Some lawyers who bill by the hour may advise against this, preferring that you fight it out in court. Just say no and get another lawyer. (Mediation and arbitration are covered in Smart Way number 2.)
- Keep roles straight. An attorney—if you decide you need one—is to advise you on the legal aspects of divorce. A therapist, counselor or minister deals with the emotional aspects. Just as you wouldn't ask a plumber to fix your teeth, don't use your attorney as your therapist. And similarly, don't decide financial issues such as how to divide a pension or value a partnership interest on the basis of emotions.

- If money is tight, check with local men's or women's support groups or the local mental health department for low cost counseling. Many therapists will offer their fees on a sliding scale if you ask.
- Take care of yourself. We take eating, sleeping and exercising for granted. Don't underestimate the importance of these to promoting a feeling of well-being during divorce. Also, avoid isolation. This is the time to rely on old friends and seek out new ones—especially people who are experiencing similar problems. The better you feel, the less likely you are to let emotions get in the way.
- Read *Learning to Leave,* by Lynette Triere (Warner Books).

RESEARCH YOUR LAWYER

When interviewing attorneys, be sure to find someone who is not threatened by a client being a *fully* informed decision maker. Take it a step further and find a lawyer who actually supports your taking an active role. Know that you do not have to use a lawyer on an all-or-nothing basis. You may be able to save time and money by doing some of the work yourself. If you plan to do much paperwork yourself, is the lawyer willing to be more of a coach than an advocate? What are the lawyer's views on mediation and do these views mesh with yours? Before engaging the services of this professional, determine the attorney's attitude and comfort level with clients who want to take an active role in their own divorces.

REACH A FEE AND
SERVICES AGREEMENT

Be sure to reach an agreement with your attorney about fees, retainers and how and when the balance of the fees will be paid. (A retainer is a sum of money, often several thousand dollars, you give the lawyer and from which the lawyer satisfies your first few bills.) The agreement should fit your finances. If you cannot meet your financial obligations to your attorney as agreed, she may discontinue services for you, leaving you the options of stopping the divorce proceedings, representing yourself or finding another attorney to represent you and paying a retainer to that attorney. A written fee agreement will prevent future misunderstandings between you and your attorney that may stall the divorce.

If you have little or no money, your spouse may be required to pay your lawyer's fees. Be sure to ask any attorney you consult about this possibility.

Don't hire the first lawyer you encounter. Shop around because fees and attitudes about fees vary. Interview several attorneys and pose the question—how can we keep costs down? Make your decision about whether and who to retain based on how well suited that attorney is to your case and how cost effective she is willing to be.

With some attorneys you *can* negotiate the fee. If you like the lawyer but the fee is too high, ask for a reduction.

Keep in mind as we've said before that you do not have to use a lawyer on an all-or-nothing basis. You can do some work yourself and then use a lawyer to check over a settlement agreement, file and serve papers and other limited tasks. One way to keep your lawyer's bill down is to only use her for legal work. If you need tax information, see an accountant or financial professional—you'll get better advice and save money by going straight to an expert in the field.

If the lawyer wants a retainer, try to convince her to reduce or forego it. If she insists, do not let the lawyer spend more than the retainer without first getting your approval. Before giving that approval, be sure you know exactly what the lawyer did in spending the retainer and what else the lawyer plans to do. Also, make sure the retainer is refundable if the lawyer doesn't do any work or you fire the lawyer before she exhausts the retainer.

There are other ways to keep fees down.

- Do some tasks yourself. You can gather documents, file papers and do other things that secretaries, paralegals or law clerks handle.
- Make sure junior lawyers or paralegals who are familiar with the divorce process and who bill at lower rates will do only routine tasks. You don't want a new lawyer with no divorce experience handling your case and learning divorce law at your expense.
- Limit the lawyers—if an associate or junior lawyer is sitting in on a meeting, be clear at the outset that you will pay for only one lawyer.
- Question the bill if something doesn't seem right.

- Provide photocopies yourself. If your lawyer needs to make copies of original documents you provide, you may be charged up to 50¢ per page!
- Insist that your attorney use regular mail rather than fax or overnight delivery for information you don't need immediately. Postage and other fees incurred by your lawyer are passed on to you. A postage stamp costs much less than $20.
- Bunch your phone calls. Your attorney may bill in six-minute segments or quarter-hour segments. Either way, you'll find that rather than calling three times and talking four minutes each, you'll save money by bunching your questions and calling just once.

**LAWYER'S RATE OF $250 PER HOUR
—BILLED IN QUARTER-HOUR INCREMENTS**

	1st call	2nd call	3rd call	Total
3 calls lasting 4 minutes each	$63	$63	$63	$189
1 call lasting 12 minutes	$63	—	—	$63

WHAT TO ASK YOUR ATTORNEY

1. How long have you practiced law and what portion of your practice is devoted to divorce cases?
2. Will I be working with you or an associate or paralegal?
3. What are your hourly rates and do you charge a retainer up front? If you don't use all of the retainer, will you refund me the unused portion?
4. When do you send bills and by when must I pay them?
5. Is your hourly rate the same or different if I need secretarial or paralegal work?
6. Who pays court fees and costs—me or my spouse? Will I have to pay my spouse's lawyer's fees (or is it possible that my spouse will have to pay mine)?
7. Do you think we'll need the help of financial experts such as an appraiser or forensic accountant?
8. Can you give me a ball park estimate of the total fee?
9. How often do your cases end in negotiated settlements versus court litigation?
10. Can you estimate how long it will take to complete my case?
11. Present company excluded, who do you think are the best matrimonial lawyers in this area?
12. Based on the information I've given you, what outcome might you expect in my case?

KEEP A TELEPHONE LOG

Make a written log of every divorce-related conversation you have with your attorney, your mediator, your spouse and your other advisors. Include in your log the date, the name of the party to whom you were speaking, and a brief but complete synopsis of what was said. This log serves as a permanent record of the progress in your divorce, and will be very helpful when memories fade or conflict. Writing each entry will help solidify the conversation in your mind. By doing this you'll avoid wasted conversations and useless avenues of pursuit. If there are disputes over time spent with an attorney or other professional, you'll have the documentation you need.

If you are going it alone, a log will be helpful in coming up with a settlement agreement as you'll see what was discussed, when, whether conclusions were reached and whether you needed to address the issue at some later time. If you are using a mediator or lawyer, the log will tell you which items have already been settled and don't need further negotiation. That will hold down professional fees.

KNOW WHAT MILITARY SPOUSES NEED TO KNOW

If you are the spouse of someone on active military duty or retired military, you need specialized knowledge as you proceed with a divorce. Knowing your rights will save you attorney's fees because you will know where, when and how to file for divorce and to what military benefits you are entitled.

To begin with, the Soldiers and Sailors Civil Relief Act, 50 U.S.C. § 501 et seq., prevents a person on active military duty from being subjected to any civil court action, including a divorce without consent. To proceed with a divorce, you will need to either secure the consent of your spouse to proceed with the divorce action, or wait until your spouse leaves active duty.

Next, you will have to decide which court has the power to hear your case. This is called jurisdiction. The court will have jurisdiction over your military spouse by reason of domicile, residence for reasons other than military service, or the military spouse's consent. For example, if you are living in New Jersey because of your spouse's military assignment but are domiciled in Texas, the Texas courts have jurisdiction, unless you and your spouse consent to have the case heard in New Jersey.

And finally, you need to know detailed information about military benefits to which you might be entitled after the divorce, including retired pay, the Survivor Benefit Plan (SBP), direct payment of alimony or child support, and medical, commissary and exchange privileges.

Military Retired Pay (Military Pensions)

Military personnel are eligible to receive retirement pay if they have served for 20 years or longer. Personnel who began service before August 1, 1986 can collect benefits equal to 50% of their pay. This percentage increases with each year served, and at 30 years of service they can collect 75% of pay. Personnel who began service on or after August 1, 1986 can retire with 40% of their pay, and at 30 years of service can collect 75% of pay.

If the military member is disabled, he will be eligible for disability pay. If the military member is terminated involuntarily due to a reduction in force, he will be eligible for a lump-sum payment, the size of which depends on the number of years he has served. If the military member is voluntarily terminated because of a reduction in force, he will receive an annuity for a number of years, again depending on the number of years he served on active duty.

The treatment of military retired pay differs from state to state. In most community property states (Arizona, California, Idaho, Louisiana, Nevada, New Mexico, Texas, Washington and Wisconsin), a portion of the military spouse's retired pay will be considered the property of both spouses, and the non-military spouse will be entitled to one-half of that portion. The portion will generally be based on the number of years of marriage during which the retired pay was earned, divided by the total years of service. If the spouses were married for at least ten years while the member was on active duty, the non-military spouse will qualify for direct enforcement, which means that her portion of the retired pay will be paid directly to her by the military finance office.

Most non-community property states will award a portion of the retired pay to the non-military spouse. A few states treat military retired pay as the property only of the military person. But usually in those states, the judge must consider the retired pay received by the military spouse when setting the amount of alimony.

A glitch in the system saves the military spouse money and is correspondingly costly to the non-military spouse. A U.S. Supreme Court decision requires that courts divide only *disposable* retired pay.[2] That means that the amount of the monthly military pension is first reduced by income tax and any other necessary withholdings. The net amount is then divided. Even if the couple was domiciled in a community property state, had been married during the entire time of service and the non-military spouse was awarded 50% of the pension by the courts, she would *actually receive less than 50%* because the monthly payment would be based on the net, rather than the gross, retirement pay.

For example, assume that the gross pay is $1,000 with $200 withheld for income taxes, leaving $800 net pay. The non-military spouse would receive one-half of the $800, or $400, and the military spouse would receive $400. Although this seems like an equal division, the inequities are obvious at tax time. The non-military spouse computes her income taxes on the $400 received, but gets no credit for withholding. This means she will owe income taxes, unless she had income taxes taken from the $400, reducing her payment even more.

The military spouse will pay tax on $600 ($1,000 gross pay, less $400 diverted to the ex-spouse), will claim the $200 of income tax withheld on his tax return, and will probably be entitled to a tax refund based on the military pay.

If you are the non-military spouse, you may wish to let your spouse keep his pension and negotiate for an item of property or investments similarly valued. Alternatively, your spouse might agree that the division of net pay is

---

[2]*Mansell vs. Mansell*, 490 U.S. 581 (1989).

not fair, and agree that you should have half of the gross retirement pay, before deductions.

If you are the military spouse, you may wish to retain all of your military benefits in exchange for giving other property to your spouse. Be aware that a division by a court would award you somewhat more of the pension than just your percentage share, as explained above. For this reason, if you and your spouse cannot agree on a division you find fair, you may want to ask a court to award the pension in accordance with the laws of your state. Obviously, that would be more expensive because it would entail going to court rather than settling the case. Weigh those costs carefully. Even if you are doing your own divorce, it may be smart to seek legal counsel on this issue.

Military Survivor Benefit Plan (SBP)

Survivor Benefit Plan survivor benefits are available to the spouse or former spouse of any retiring member.

Under the Survivor Benefit Plan, a retiring member's spouse will be enrolled automatically for survivor benefits unless the member and his spouse agree in writing to reduce or waive the coverage. Full survivor benefits equal 55% of the gross retired pay until age 62, at which time the benefits drop, due to an offset for Social Security benefits received by the survivor. The cost of the coverage is generally 6.5% of the retired pay, with certain adjustments made for retirees who receive less than $720 in retirement pay per month.

When a retired military member divorces, he is required to notify the appropriate Finance Center which handles pay for his branch of the military. The military will terminate the coverage under SBP, and he will receive a refund for all payments that he made for coverage since the divorce. If he remarries, the new spouse will become automatically covered after one year of marriage.

A special rule allows the retiree to reinstate his former spouse (and minor children) as beneficiaries, if both spouses sign a reinstatement application and submit it to the appropriate Finance Center within one year of the date of divorce.

Similarly, an active duty member may agree to name his ex-spouse as beneficiary of the SBP when he retires.[3] Both spouses must sign a written notarized agreement and incorporate it into the divorce decree.

If you are the military spouse and your spouse requests to be named as beneficiary on a life insurance policy (see Smart Way number 67), you may find it more advantageous to name your former spouse as beneficiary under SBP than to purchase the life insurance she requests. The cost of the SBP coverage may be lower than the cost of life insurance, and the amount withheld for the SBP coverage is tax deductible.

If you are the non-military spouse, you will find that the cost-of-living increases in the SBP are a definite advantage over life insurance, which has no cost of living adjustments. The investment income that you would receive on life insurance benefits paid to you in a lump sum, however, may outweigh the cost of living benefits of the SBP, making the life insurance coverage preferable. You may also prefer receiving a lump-sum payment of life insurance over the monthly SBP payments, because at your death, any money you have remaining from the life insurance proceeds can be passed to your heirs, while the SBP benefits die with you.

Direct Payment of Child Support and Alimony

If a valid court order is presented to the Finance Center which handles pay for your branch of the military, alimony and child support will be withheld from the military spouse's pay and then paid directly to the ex-spouse once a month.

---

[3] *10 U.S.C. §1450(f)(4).*

The supported spouse will receive payments at the end of the month rather than at the beginning of the month or twice a month, as is customary with support. This is because the support will be withheld from the pay of the military spouse, and will not be paid over until withholding of the full month has been made. If your spouse can be trusted, you may find it beneficial to forego direct payment by the military, and rather have him pay you himself each time he receives a paycheck.

Medical, Commissary, and Exchange Privileges

Full medical, commissary and exchange privileges are available to an ex-spouse if the military member served 20 years, and the spouses were married for 20 years while the member was on active duty. If the military member served 20 years and the spouses were married for 20 years, but the member was on active duty only 15 to 19 of those years during the marriage, the ex-spouse will be entitled only to medical care for a limited period of time (with certain exceptions for divorces finalized before April 1, 1985). After that limited time, she will have 90 days to enroll in a group health plan established by the Department of Defense. If she remarries, she loses all her privileges.

A divorced spouse is not entitled to medical, commissary or exchange privileges if the marriage was fewer than 20 years or the military spouse served fewer than 20 years.

HELP FOR SPOUSES OF MILITARY PERSONNEL

If you are divorcing a military spouse, join EX-POSE and request the booklet *A Guide for Military Wives Facing Separatrion or Divorce*. Information is available from:

    EX-POSE
    P.O. Box 11191
    Alexandria, VA 22312
    713-255-2917 or 713-941-5844

PART 2

SAVING ON ALIMONY

Alimony may not be an issue in your divorce. If yours is a short marriage, you are both working, self-supporting and in good health, then neither of you will need or be entitled to alimony. In New York state, for example, alimony is awarded in only 15% of all divorces. Even if one of you will receive alimony, chances are it will be for only a few years—until the children are in school full-time or the supported ex-spouse obtains job training or finishes school and enters or re-enters the job market.

In most states, when alimony is awarded, it is based on such factors as each person's needs and earning capabilities, the age, health and standard of living of each person, the length of the marriage and the tax advantages and disadvantages of paying or receiving alimony.

In this section, we offer tips for those spouses who will include alimony (called maintenance or spousal support in some states) as a part of their divorce. By documenting living expenses and identifying all income sources, you can maximize what you will receive or minimize what you will pay. By understanding the tax implications of paying and receiving alimony— including when it might be advantageous to alter the taxability of your alimony award—you can save money. We highlight some special tax traps regarding the alimony tax deduction and a relatively new and sophisticated technique called an alimony substitution trust.

UNDERSTAND THE FINANCIAL BENEFITS OF BEING MARRIED TEN YEARS

In some states, such as California, in a marriage of ten years or longer, the court retains the right to order that alimony be paid to the lesser-earning spouse for as long as she needs it, if the other spouse has the ability to pay. If you do not know the rules in your state, you could unintentionally lose your right to alimony. For instance, you and your spouse might negotiate a fixed amount of alimony for a set period. If you designate that alimony as non-modifiable in your settlement agreement, the court will not retain the right to extend alimony beyond the time specified, even if your marriage was longer than ten years. Similarly, you and your spouse may include a mutual waiver of alimony in your divorce agreement. If you waive your right to alimony, you can't get it back, even if your marriage lasted more than ten years.

DOCUMENT LIVING EXPENSES

What is the cost of the lifestyle you have lived during your married life? Whether you are paying or receiving alimony, whether you are going it alone or working with an attorney or mediator, you will probably have to complete and submit to the court a form documenting your income and expenses.

Here are major categories of monthly expenses:

- Residence payments (rent or mortgage, taxes and insurance, maintenance)
- Food at home and household supplies
- Food eating out
- Utilities
- Telephone
- Laundry and cleaning
- Clothing
- Medical and dental (insurance and out of pocket payments)
- Insurance (life and accident)
- Child care
- Education
- Entertainment
- Transportation and auto expenses (insurance, gas, oil and repairs)
- Installment payments (credit cards and loans)
- Incidentals

By carefully documenting living expenses, you may receive more alimony if you are the recipient or pay less alimony if you are the payer. If you are negotiating your alimony, this information will help you justify to your spouse why you should receive more. Likewise, if you are paying alimony, a clear picture of your expenses may help your spouse understand and accept payments that are lower than she might have anticipated.

An attorney will use this information in much the same way—to attempt to satisfy the needs of one spouse while not bankrupting the other.

IDENTIFY ALL INCOME

Alimony is computed taking into account a variety of factors, the most important of which is the income of the parties from all sources. For that reason, identifying all income received by both parties is very important. You will save money if you and your spouse do this yourselves, rather than paying your lawyer to compile it item by item.

Start with your federal income tax return and total up your taxable income. Then add to that total any additional non-taxable income.

Taxable Income

Here are several common sources of taxable income. Refer to Appendix A for an exhaustive list of sources of taxable income.

- Armed Forces pay (except combat or missing status pay)
- Barter income
- Business profits
- Commissions
- Dividends on stocks and mutual funds paid from income or capital gains
- Farm income
- Gain on sale of property, patents, goodwill, stock, bonds, etc.
- Hobby income
- Income from Subchapter S corporations
- Income tax refunds from state, if previously deducted
- Interest on bank deposits, bonds, judgments, condemnation awards, federal obligations, insurance contracts, federal tax refunds
- Jury pay
- Mileage allowance
- Military per diem pay
- Pension distributions attributable to employer contributions
- Professional fees
- Rents
- Royalties and advances against royalties
- Salaries and wages
- Tips
- Unemployment benefits

Non-Taxable Income

Some income you receive is not taxable. Below you will find several common sources of non-taxable income. A more complete list appears in Appendix B.

- Accident and health insurance paid by your employer
- Car pool receipts by car owner from fellow employees

- Car furnished to full-time car salesperson used for business
- Child care plan benefits subsidized by employer
- Child support payments
- Disability payments for personal injuries or sickness, including Veterans' Administration payments
- Dividends from stock that represent a return of capital
- Educational assistance provided by employer, up to $5,250
- Fellowships and scholarships for degree programs
- Foreign earned income (limited)
- Foster parents reimbursement for care of foster child
- Interest from municipal bonds
- Juror's mileage allowance
- Lodging and meals furnished for employer's convenience
- Social Security or Railroad Retirement payments below base amount

If the income and expenses from a business are reported on your tax return, be aware that not all the expenses shown for the business require out-of-pocket money, so the net income may be higher than shown. For instance, depreciation, though a legitimate claim against gross income for tax purposes, merely reflects the aging of an asset owned and does not reflect a real outlay of cash. Similarly, the tax laws allow a business owner to deduct up to $17,500 of equipment in the year it was purchased, even though it will last for a number of years. The cost of that equipment should not be considered when calculating the net income from the business, given that the equipment will not need replacement for years to come.

Sometimes, deductions are claimed on an income tax return for costs associated with a home office. These expenses appear on Form 8829, Expenses for Business Use of Your Home. Although those costs are legitimate tax deductions, some of them would be continuing and personal in nature were the business not owned, and should not be considered as expenses for the purposes of calculating net income from the business. Similarly, some of the travel and entertainment deducted on a business tax return may be personal in nature, as the trip would have been taken anyway or the meal eaten if the business did not exist. A portion of automobile expenses may fall into the same category. If you will be receiving alimony, it is in your best interest to investigate these issues. You may want to ask your tax professional or accountant to help you through the process.

To identify such expenses for an unincorporated business, look on Schedule C, Profit or Loss from Business, where business income and expenses are reported. To the line "Net profit or (loss)," add back any amounts for which the owner received personal benefit, such as travel, meals and entertainment, car and truck expense for personal use of business car, depreciation, personal telephone expenses and the like. For farm income, you would do the same using Schedule F, Profit or Loss From Farming.

For a partnership, begin with the income shown on Schedule K-1, Partner's Share of Income, Credits, Deductions, Etc., on line J(c), and then add back the partner's share of any personal benefit items deducted on page one of Form 1065, U.S. Partnership Income Tax Return. For a corporation, begin with the line "Taxable income before net operating loss deduction and special deductions" on page one of Form 1120, U.S. Corporation Income Tax Return, or the line "Ordinary income (loss) from trade or business activities" on Form 1120S, U.S. Income Tax Return for an S Corporation. Add back any amounts claimed for which the shareholder received a personal economic benefit.

In addition to the categories above, look also for interest paid to the shareholder, charitable contributions on behalf of the shareholder, and pension and profit sharing contributions and employee benefit programs for the benefit of the shareholder. Schedule L will show any loans made to the shareholder, which represent cash but were not taxed to him. Look also at

Schedule M-1 for income recorded on the books but not included on the tax return, such as tax-exempt interest.

Identifying unreported income will not only help you calculate support, but it can also affect the value of the business. (See Smart Ways number 45 and 46.)

HELP FROM A FORENSIC ACCOUNTANT

A forensic accountant is usually a Certified Public Accountant who has investigatory skills and expertise in the financial aspects of law. A good forensic accountant will sift methodically through past accounts and records and piece together what is usually an accurate picture of one's financial position. Forensic accountants generally have considerable experience testifying in court cases. Ask an attorney for a recommendation of qualified forensic accountants.

When computing the income from a business, be alert for signs of missing income which should have been reported on the tax returns or financial statements, but which was not. If you suspect that there is missing income, a forensic accountant can help you discover the missing income.

BE SURE YOUR ALIMONY MEETS TAX DEDUCTION REQUIREMENTS

Can you deduct the alimony, maintenance or spousal support you will pay? Must you pay taxes on the support you will receive? The basic answer is yes. In general, alimony is treated as taxable income to the person receiving it and as a tax deduction to the person paying it, but only if the payments meet the Five Ds for deduction of alimony—dollars, document, distance, death and designation.

Dollars

The payment must be made in cash, not property or services, to or on behalf of the receiving ex-spouse. Payments made to a third party by one ex-spouse on behalf of the other will qualify as deductible alimony, but not if the payment benefits the paying party.

For example, if you make mortgage payments on the house which you own but in which your ex-spouse resides, that payment won't qualify as alimony because you are making the payment on your own behalf, as owner. You may be able to claim the interest as a deduction on your tax return as interest paid on a second residence, however. On the other hand, if you make the car payment on a car owned by your ex-spouse, and that payment is called for in your divorce decree, then the payment will qualify as deductible alimony, and will be taxable income to your ex.

Document

The payment must be made under a decree of divorce or separate maintenance, a written separation agreement or other decree requiring support payments. If there is no such agreement or decree, payments from one ex-spouse to the other won't be tax deductible (or includable in income by the other ex-spouse). This can come as a real surprise to the paying spouse, who was anticipating an income tax deduction.

If you are paying alimony to your soon-to-be ex-spouse and the two of you are not planning to file a joint return or will be ineligible to do so, you will want to get a written separation agreement or decree ordering support as soon as possible so that payments made after that date will be deductible by you. If you are the spouse receiving payments, however, it will be to your advantage to keep matters informal, and to delay a written agreement or decree. But remember that you cannot enforce the support payments unless you have an agreement or decree, so consider the consequences of informal arrangements carefully.

Distance

If payment is made under a decree of divorce or separate maintenance, the parties cannot be members of the same household when payments are made. If you continue living with your ex-spouse after divorce or legal separation, payments for alimony won't be deductible by the payer nor taxable to the recipient. After the divorce or legal separation is final, you have one month from the date of the first payment for one of you to move out and still satisfy this requirement.

Death

Alimony will not be deductible to the payer if he is required to make payments even after the recipient ex-spouse dies. If the divorce decree orders payments to be made to the recipient's estate or heirs after the recipient's death, *none* of the payments will be deductible by the payer or taxable to the recipient.

Designation

Alimony will not be deductible if the payments are designated as child support or are designated as non-deductible and non-taxable. If you have provided in your divorce decree that future payments will not be taxable or deductible, then they will not be taxable regardless of the fact that they meet the other four Ds for deduction.

CALLING CHILD SUPPORT ALIMONY COULD SAVE YOU TAXES

Child support is not deductible. In families where the payer is in a higher tax bracket than the recipient, it may make sense to call some of that child support alimony. The government would receive less in taxes if more money were shifted through alimony from the payer's higher tax bracket to the recipient's lower tax bracket.

If your agreement with your spouse is that alimony and child support will end at different times, you'll need to pay attention to the child support you are calling alimony. The recharacterized support may end sooner than intended if your child is still very young, or last longer than desired if your child is near 18.

If you want to shift the tax burden for *all* of the child support and alimony to the recipient, consider combining the two payments into one. This is discussed more fully at Smart Way number 19. In either case, make sure you don't fall into one of the alimony traps discussed in Smart Way number 17.

BEWARE OF ALIMONY DEDUCTION TAX TRAPS

As mentioned above, alimony must comply with the Five Ds for Deduction in order for it to be taxable to the receiving ex-spouse and deductible by the payer. But even if it does qualify under the Five Ds, there are two special tax traps to nab the unwary.

Reductions related to children. Because alimony is deductible by the payer and child support is not, people sometimes characterize otherwise non-deductible child support as alimony or undifferentiated family support (see Smart Way number 19) in the divorce decree. In that case, the decree usually provides for a decrease in "alimony" when the child or children reach majority. If your divorce decree provides that alimony will decrease or terminate upon an event relating to a child, such as the child reaching a certain age, marrying, dying, leaving school, becoming employed or moving out, the amount of the reduction in alimony will be treated as child support. It is not legal to deduct it as alimony, regardless of its characterization in the divorce decree.

Similarly, if the alimony is to decrease on a certain date, and that date is within six months before or after your child reaches the age of majority in your state (18 or 21), that decrease is considered disguised child support and cannot legally be deducted by the payer. The rules are somewhat more complex and equally as strict if the decree calls for two or more reductions because of several minor children.

The simplest way to comply with these rules is to characterize child support as child support in your separation agreement, and accept that it is neither deductible to the payer nor taxable to the recipient. If you are determined to make the child support deductible/taxable, you should not mention any planned decreases in alimony in your divorce decree, so you will not run afoul of IRS regulations. You and your spouse can renegotiate the support in future years—but beware of alimony recapture provisions, discussed below.

Alternatively, your separation agreement can specify that the higher alimony payments will continue until a date that is at least six months after your child reaches the age of majority. If you need two or more reductions because you have two or more children, you may have to extend the higher alimony payments even longer.

Alimony recapture provisions. Alimony recapture provisions were enacted to prevent couples from disguising otherwise non-deductible property settlement payments as deductible alimony. Alimony that meets the Five Ds for Deduction still falls afoul of the alimony recapture provisions if alimony payments decrease by $15,000 or more from one year to the next during the first three years after divorce.

For example, if you paid $50,000 in alimony in the first year, $30,000 in the second year and $10,000 in the third year, you would be subject to the recapture provisions at the end of the third year. (Recapture is computed only at the end of the third year, even if the drop from year one to two is $15,000 or more.) Using a complex formula, alimony recapture (additional income reported on the payer's tax return for the third year after divorce that he earlier deducted) of $17,500 would be computed. In the third year after divorce, the payer would report $17,500 of additional income on his income tax return due to that recapture, and the recipient ex-spouse would have a corresponding deduction on her tax return.

This would be the result even if the reductions in the second or third year were not called for in the divorce decree. If the decree called for $50,000 alimony every year, but the payer became delinquent and thus made the lower payments, the alimony recapture rules would come into play. Similarly, if the parties renegotiated or the court changed the agreement in the second or third year, the alimony recapture rules would still take effect. The only exceptions to the rules are if either party dies or the recipient remarries.

A common situation in which divorcing couples run afoul of the alimony recapture rules is when one spouse agrees to pay the attorney's fees of the other spouse, but wants the payment to be described as additional alimony so that he can deduct the payment on his tax return. If the payment exceeds $15,000, he may be subject to recapture provisions.

You may not have a problem if the divorce occurs part way through a calendar year, because the alimony paid after the divorce and before December 31 will not be as great as if the divorce occurred at the beginning of the year. In that case, paying additional alimony during the first calendar year after divorce may not cause a problem.

If alimony payments will decrease during the first three years after divorce, there are two things you can do to avoid recapture:

- Consider making a partial payment the first year, and deferring the rest of the payment to another calendar year. For example, assume your intended agreement was to make alimony payments of $50,000 the first year, $30,000 the second year, and $10,000 the third year. As we said above, this would result in $17,500 recapture income in the third year. If you postpone paying $15,000 of the intended first year payment until the third year, payments will be $35,000, $30,000 and $25,000. You will eliminate recapture, as the reduction will have been less than $15,000 between any two years.

- Remain aware of the potential problem of alimony recapture, and ask an accountant to review the provisions of your decree before you sign it to make sure you are effectively circumventing the complex alimony recapture provisions.

Consider Making Alimony Non-Taxable

While alimony is generally taxable to the person receiving it and deductible by the person paying it, you have another option. If the after-divorce tax bracket of the payer is lower than the after-divorce tax bracket of the recipient, it may be to your advantage to make alimony non-taxable. Although it would be unusual for this to be the case based solely on the gross incomes of the payer and recipient, it might be the case if the payer has many tax deductions, credits or loss carryovers. Have your tax adviser calculate which strategy would give you the greater overall tax savings.

Alimony that would ordinarily be taxable to the recipient and deductible by the payer can be made non-taxable and non-deductible by simply stating so in your divorce decree or in a writing that refers to the divorce decree. The ex-spouse *receiving* the support must attach the written statement to her income tax return.

Usually, the decision is made at the time of divorce for all years alimony will be paid. You can, however, specify in your divorce decree that you will make the decision annually. Your divorce decree would state that your alimony will follow the traditional rules of being taxable to the recipient and deductible by the payer unless both of you specify in writing that treatment for a particular year will be different. Consider this kind option if one or both of you expect your incomes and deductions to fluctuate year to year.

For example, if the recipient is generally in a lower tax bracket than the payer, then in most years you would treat the alimony as deductible and taxable. In a particular year, however, the paying ex-spouse may incur losses, such as a business loss or casualty loss, that lowers his tax bracket or even eliminates his taxable income altogether. Because he needs no additional deductions that year, the recipient would save income taxes if you called the alimony non-deductible by him and non-taxable to his ex-spouse. To make the deal advantageous for both, they could split her tax savings.

When to Make Alimony Non-Taxable

Here are some examples of situations in which non-taxable/non-deductible alimony will save income taxes.

To Absorb Unusual Losses in an Ex-Spouse's Return
- The paying ex-spouse has net operating losses in his business which exceed the amount he can use this year or carry back to prior years. He therefore can't use the alimony deduction.
- The paying ex-spouse has accumulated suspended passive activity losses from his tax-sheltered investments, such as investment partner-

ships or real estate. Under current tax law, those losses can be deducted only in years in which he has income from such investments. The amounts not deductible each year are suspended, and the accumulated suspended losses can be deducted in the year you sell or dispose of your investment. In that year, he probably won't need the alimony deduction.

- The paying ex-spouse has a large casualty loss which exceeds his income for current year. He can't use the alimony deduction this year.

To Reduce the Effect of Reduction Floors

- The receiving ex-spouse has large medical expenses that exceed the deduction floor of 7.5% of her income. Non-taxable alimony would reduce her income and increase her medical deduction, thus saving taxes owed.
- The receiving ex-spouse has large employee business expenses, job-hunting expenses, deductible portion of legal services relating to her divorce, or other miscellaneous deductions that exceed the deduction floor of 2% of her income. Non-taxable alimony would reduce her income and increase her miscellaneous deductions.

To Reduce "Phase Out" for Certain Deductions

- The receiving ex-spouse is eligible for the earned income credit or child care credit, which becomes less as income increases. Electing out of taxation of alimony will lower her income and increase her allowable credits.
- The receiving ex-spouse has rental real estate losses which are limited if her income exceeds $100,000. If her income, including alimony, would exceed that amount, electing out of taxable alimony would reduce her income and allow her a greater real estate activity deduction.

- The paying ex-spouse earns more than the amount at which personal exemptions are phased out (over $234,300 in 1994). The receiving ex-spouse is at the beginning of the phase out ($111,800 in 1994). Electing out of taxation of alimony will reduce the receiving ex-spouse's income and prevent phase out on her return.
- The paying ex-spouse has income so high that he has lost 80% of his itemized deductions through the limitations (3% of income over $111,800 for 1994). If the receiving ex-spouse's income is over the threshold amount ($111,800 for 1994), non-taxable alimony will reduce her income and increase her deductible itemized deductions.

To Eliminate or Reduce Taxes on Income

- Because children under 14 must pay tax at the custodial parent's rate for all income over $1,200 the children receive, making alimony non-taxable may reduce the custodial parent's income tax bracket and therefore the tax the child would pay. This obviously is a concern only if your children have a lot of income, as would be the case if they are beneficiaries of a trust, budding rock stars or Anna Paquin.
- If the receiving ex-spouse has invested in U.S. Savings Bonds for her child's education and will cash them in this year, and if her income is over $45,500, she will have to pay tax on a portion of the bond interest. Electing to make alimony non-taxable will reduce her income and may eliminate the tax on the bond interest.
- If the receiving ex-spouse collects Social Security, she will pay tax on a portion of it if her income exceeds $25,000. By making alimony non-taxable, her income may fall below that threshold and eliminate the taxation of her Social Security benefits.
- If the paying ex-spouse is subject to alternate minimum tax and the receiving ex-spouse is in a bracket higher than that, electing out of

taxation of alimony will cause income to be taxed at the paying spouse's lower rate.

TAXABLE AND NON-TAXABLE ALIMONY— KEY COMPARISONS

If you pay taxable alimony, you:
- Receive deduction for alimony paid
- See advantages if you are a high income earner
- Can include insurance premiums and other payments and get a tax deduction

If you pay non-taxable alimony:
- You have no deductions for the alimony
- Both parties must agree
- You must state it in writing
- You can do on a year-by-year basis
- There may be more after-tax dollars to split

If you receive taxable alimony, you:
- Pay taxes on alimony income
- Can make deductible IRA contributions from alimony received

If you receive non-taxable alimony:
- It does not increase your tax liability
- Both parties must agree
- You must state it in writing
- You can do on a year-by-year basis
- There may be more after-tax dollars to split

CONSIDER FAMILY SUPPORT AS AN ALTERNATIVE TO ALIMONY AND CHILD SUPPORT

Unlike alimony, child support is neither taxable to the recipient nor deductible by the payer. If you combine the alimony and child support payments into something called undifferentiated family support or family maintenance, the entire payment will be taxable to the recipient and deductible by the payer.

Courts sometimes award, or parties sometimes agree to, undifferentiated family support because it saves income taxes if the payer is in a higher income tax bracket than the recipient. Because undifferentiated support will save overall income taxes, the payer generally makes higher payments to cover the additional income taxes that the recipient will owe and to share the overall tax savings.

Although courts in the past have ordered family support, the practice is dying out. Because child support cannot be distinguished from alimony when they are combined, government officials who collect delinquent child support payments have had trouble enforcing family support orders. In addition, most states now require that support orders specify the amount for child support for each child, thus eliminating the use of undifferentiated orders.

PLAN AHEAD FOR THE TAXES YOU'LL OWE
OR THE PAYMENTS YOU'LL MAKE

Whether you'll be making alimony payments or paying income taxes on the alimony you receive, you will need to make adjustments in the taxes you pay. If you fail to make those adjustments, it will cost the recipient tax penalties for underpayment of taxes. At the same time, the payer will have excess taxes withheld from his salary or will overpay his quarterly estimated tax.

If you are the payer, you can increase the number of withholding allowances that you claim on the W-4 form that you file with your employer. You can claim one additional withholding allowance for each $2,500 of deductible alimony you pay each year. By claiming additional withholding allowances, you will increase the size of your paycheck, giving you more money from which to make the alimony payments.

If you fail to increase your withholding allowances, you can still claim a deduction on your income tax return for the alimony you paid. But by failing to increase your withholding allowances to reflect your alimony payments, you will have had extra taxes withheld. Any income tax refund to which you are entitled will be increased; any income taxes you owe will be decreased. If you are self-employed and make quarterly estimated income tax payments, include the deduction for alimony payments in your calculations.

If you receive alimony, and your total annual income exceeds $6,250, you will have to pay taxes on your income, including the alimony you receive. The government requires that the taxes you owe on the alimony be paid in quarterly estimated tax payments, due on April 15, June 15, September 15 and January 15 of the following year. Alternatively, if you are employed, you can ask your employer to increase the withholding from your paycheck to cover the additional taxes due on the alimony. File a new W-4 withholding allowance form with your employer directing that additional taxes be withheld from each paycheck.

To compute the amount of estimated tax payments or extra withholding required, jot your estimate of this year's income and deductions in the margin of a copy of last year's income tax return. Using the tax rates for the current year (see the instructions for Form 1040-ES for estimated tax payments), calculate the taxes on your estimated taxable income. Subtract from that amount your estimate of withholding for the year and estimated tax payments already made. The result is the additional taxes you will owe for the year. Divide that amount by the remaining estimated tax installment dates, or by the number of pay periods remaining for the year. That figure is the amount of estimated tax you must pay for each remaining installment of estimated tax, or the amount of extra withholding you should request your employer to withhold.

Although making accurate calculations is important, the IRS does allow you some room for error. But if you fail to pay at least 90% of the income taxes you will owe for the year through withholding and estimated tax payments, you will incur a tax penalty for failure to pay estimated income taxes. There are two exceptions to this rule. You will owe no penalty if the balance due is less than $500. Also, you will owe no penalty if your withholding plus estimated tax payments for the year equal 100% (110% for individuals whose income exceeds $150,000) of the total tax owed for the prior year.

CONSIDER AN ALIMONY SUBSTITUTION TRUST

Alimony substitution trusts have become increasingly popular among the well-to-do since the tax laws governing such trusts were streamlined in 1984. Although the use of a trust to pay alimony is more cumbersome than direct payments, it can help satisfy psychological needs of both ex-spouses and substitute as an estate-planning device if the trust assets will be left to children or to charity. Also, because the payments come from a trust and not directly from the payer, they are considered trust income, not alimony, and can help you circumvent some sticky parts of the tax law.

If your ex-spouse is required to pay alimony and has income-producing assets such as brokerage accounts or rental real estate, consider using an alimony substitution trust. The payer sets up a trust, naming a bank trust department or another independent party as trustee. He transfers assets into the trust to produce sufficient income to fund the required alimony payment. Each month the trustee sends a distribution directly to the recipient. Annual trustee costs vary according to locale and amount of trust principal, but generally range from 0.75% to 2.00% of trust assets.

The major advantage to the recipient is that she does not have to depend on her ex to send a check every month. As long as the trust contains sufficient assets to make the payments, she will get them on time.

The major advantages to the payer are that he is relieved of the bother of writing a check each month and can put more psychological distance between himself and his ex. When his obligation to pay alimony ends, the trust can be terminated and ownership of the assets in trust will revert back to him.

The alimony substitution trust gets around some sticky parts of the tax law:

- Because the payments from trust income are not technically alimony, they are not subject to the three year recapture rule for excessive front-loading of payments. See Smart Way number 17 for discussion of the three year recapture rule.

- Because the payments are a distribution of trust income, the provisions that require that amounts designated as alimony be treated as child support if reductions in support related to the child occur do not have any effect on the taxability/deductibility of the payment. Again, see Smart Way number 17 for more on this.

Alimony Substitution Trust and Direct Alimony Payments Compared

Recipient

- The income received is trust income, not alimony income. It is still taxable, but you cannot make IRA contributions using it. (Smart Way number 70 covers using alimony to make IRA contributions.)

- Because the payments aren't alimony, you and your ex cannot specifically elect to make the payments non-taxable to you and non-deductible by your ex, as you can with alimony. (Smart Way number 18 covers making alimony non-taxable.)

Payer

- Because the payments are trust income, not alimony, you will not receive a deduction for alimony paid. But because you are transferring pretaxed income to your ex-spouse, your ex-spouse pays income tax on it while you do not have to report it as taxable income. The net effect on your taxable income is the same as if you paid alimony and deducted it.

- If you place insufficient assets in the trust, the trust will not generate enough income (interest, dividends, rents and the like) to satisfy your support obligation. If the trustee must use trust *principal* to make the payment, you will not be able to deduct the payment and your ex will not owe taxes on it. To prevent this, make sure the trust agreement states that:

  ✓ trust payments will be made from income only
  ✓ the trustee will alert you if the principal is not generating enough income to cover your alimony payments, and
  ✓ you will be obligated to make up any shortfall from other sources.

PART 3

PAYING AND RECEIVING
CHILD SUPPORT PAINLESSLY

When a marriage ends, you cease being husband and wife, but your roles as parents continue if you have children. Discussions about custody and child support often touch deep nerves. Anger over these issues can lead to protracted negotiations and non-compliance with agreements. This will result in high attorney's fees and court costs, and wasted time and money. Dollars can be saved for the benefit of children and parents when both ex-spouses are committed to their roles as mother and father and have a clear understanding of the rationale behind the guidelines for child support.

In this section, we'll help you anticipate your child support obligation or award by better understanding your state's guidelines and support formulas, documenting your income and children's needs, and taking into account expenses not in the formula. The purpose of child support is to ensure that your children's needs are adequately met, and that they don't become economic victims of divorce, or dependent on government assistance for their welfare.

We'll also discuss the reasons why you'll want to keep a calendar of when your children are with each parent. Some parents interfere with visitation when child support is late or non-existent. You'll learn why this isn't a good idea. You'll also discover that including a COLA (cost-of-living adjustment) clause can save you money.

No matter how much child support you will pay or receive, remember that it is neither taxable to the recipient it nor deductible to payer unless it is combined with alimony and called family support. (See Smart Way number 19.)

UNDERSTAND YOUR STATE'S GUIDELINES FOR SETTING CHILD SUPPORT—DOCUMENT YOUR INCOME AND CHILDREN'S NEEDS

Two federal laws of the 1980s require all states to enact guidelines for determining child support.[4] Although Congress did not direct the type of guidelines to be used, most states rely on two factors—the parent's ability to pay and the child's needs.

The guidelines vary from state to state. Some states consider the net income of only the noncustodial parent. Most states, however, consider the net income of both parents. Some states consider the income of a new spouse or live-in mate—that income might relieve the expenses of the parent, thereby making more money available to the payer to pay child support, or reducing the recipient's need for child support. Also, some states factor in the

---

[4]Child Support Enforcement Act of 1984 (42 U.S.C. 651 and following) and Family Support Act of 1988 (42 U.S.C § 666)

amount of time the child spends with each parent. Other states ignore the fact that a noncustodial parent may spend more time with a child than just limited visitation or that the parents may actually share custody of the children.

Courts generally have the power to order additional support if the child has extraordinary expenses relating to education or health care. Also, most states require that the formula consider two additional factors: support paid for children from another relationship and child care expenses the custodial parent incurs to work or attend school. A few states increase child support to take into consideration the extracurricular activities of your children.

A few states consider (and therefore reduce the basic amount of child support) if the payer has business or personal educational expenses, has suffered catastrophic loss or has heavy debts or other pressing cash needs. But not all states permit a reduction for these reasons, favoring the payment of child support before considering any financial hardships. And many states permit a lower child support award than what's required under the formula if *both* parents agree to it and the child will be adequately supported.

To compute the amount required by your state on your own, you will need a copy of your state's formula. Call the court clerk to see if it's available at the clerk's office. If it's not, a divorce typing service, a women's or men's support group or an attorney should have a copy. Most lawyers and family court judges agree that the amount determined by the formula is the amount the court orders to be paid in 75% of all child support cases.

The first key to paying or receiving the appropriate amount of child support is to accurately calculate your and your soon-to-be ex-spouse's income. For more information on documenting income, refer to Smart Way number 15.

The second key is to document the extraordinary and extracurricular needs of your children that your state factors into the child support formula. Consider all possible orthodontic work, reading tutors, vacations, sports lessons, therapy and whatever else you can think of. Make sure that your settlement agreement specifies which additional expenses will be included in your child support formula. This will prevent future court battles and expensive attorney fees to resolve disputes.

CONSIDER EXPENSES NOT FACTORED INTO THE CHILD SUPPORT FORMULA

As mentioned above, about 75% of all child support awards are simply the amount determined by the state formula. In the other 25% of cases, the presence of any of the following issues may result in a departure from the formula:

- Either parent has remarried or has a live-in mate.
- The noncustodial parent's income is extraordinarily high.
- The noncustodial parent would be left with an unreasonably low amount of money to live on.

These issues present grounds for deviating from the formula. In addition, parents will want to address financial matters that go beyond the scope of the formula. In fact, in some states, parents must make arrangements for the following non-formula expenses:

- Who will maintain health insurance for the children?

- How will other medical expenses and deductibles be paid—shared equally, shared in certain percentages or by one parent only?
- How will any therapy or substance abuse treatment be paid—shared equally, shared in certain percentages or by one parent only? (This is in addition to the above question because some states do not include therapy in the definition of medical expenses.)
- How will special school expenses, such as sports uniforms and equipment, activity fees and group trips be paid—shared equally, shared in certain percentages or by one parent only? Because some parents disagree on the need for these expenses, consider agreeing in writing to mediate any disagreements over your children's school activities and the costs associated with them. Bear in mind that an agreement specifying who will pay these costs could be hard to enforce. A court may not be willing to enforce more than the basic child support requirement.
- How will future college costs be paid? You should negotiate the financial responsibility for higher education as part of your settlement agreement. Again, understand that a negotiated agreement for college education of children may not be enforceable.
- If one of you dies, how will your minor children's expenses be met? Do you each have sufficient money to leave in a trust for their benefit? If not, you may want to require at least one parent to maintain a life insurance policy for the benefit of the children.

KEEP A CALENDAR OF WHEN YOUR CHILDREN ARE WITH EACH PARENT

Keeping a calendar of the days (and nights) your child spends at your house and your ex-spouse's house is important for two reasons.

First, if your state includes in the computation of child support the percentage of time the child spends with each parent, a calendar marked will show indisputably when the child was where. This will help you negotiate the initial amount of child support and subsequent modifications.

Second, a calendar will be helpful if the IRS requires you to prove your right to claim head of household filing status. (See Smart Way number 62.)

DON'T INTERFERE WITH VISITATION

If you receive child support, don't jeopardize your ex-spouse's prompt payment each month by interfering with visitation rights or by criticizing him to your children or to his family and friends. Studies have shown that the more connection a noncustodial parent feels with his children, the more likely he is to pay child support on a regular and continuing basis.

If your spouse falls behind in child support, it is still a mistake to withhold visitation. Courts consider child support and visitation separate and distinct rights. Legally and practically, you want to reinforce, not weaken, the bond between the noncustodial parent and your children. Your refusal to let your ex-spouse see the children will cause hard feelings and make him even more reluctant to pay support. Furthermore, if you interfere with his right to visitation, he can take you to court. You could be held in contempt of court and fined, and have to pay his attorney fees to boot. If you withhold visitation, the courts will not look favorably upon you. And if your interference is gross, such as kidnapping the children or concealing them from your ex-spouse, the courts may change custody of the children or possibly relieve your ex of the obligation to pay child support.

Of course, if you fear that your ex-spouse is on drugs or drinking when with the children, is abusive or otherwise dangerous to your children's well-being, take immediate legal steps. Petition the court for an order either to deny visitation or to allow supervised visitation in the presence of a third party or at a courthouse visitation room.

INCLUDE A COLA
(COST OF LIVING ADJUSTMENT) CLAUSE

Most child support awards call for a set amount with no provisions for automatic increases in the future. But it is expensive for you and your ex-spouse to go back to court for a modification. In addition, going to court for a modification can lead to hard feelings between the two of you, and often between you and your children. After all, if the custodial parent is feeling a monetary pinch and files papers with the court for more support, the older children will probably be aware of the legal action. If the paying parent puts up a fight, the children may get angry, feel abandoned or feel that the noncustodial parent doesn't love them.

To deal with these problems in advance, and to avoid them cropping up later, consider including a cost of living adjustment clause in your settlement agreement. This will ensure that the support you receive or pay will support your children adequately, as inflation erodes its buying power. For example, you might agree to something like this:

It is further agreed that the amount of support to be paid each month shall be adjusted annually to reflect any increase or decrease in the cost of living. This adjustment shall take into account the cost of living in the City of _____ on the date of this agreement, and the cost of living on each anniversary of this agreement in the city where the custodial parent may then reside. The basis of this computation shall be the "Consumer Price Index—Cities, published by the Bureau of Labor Statistics of the U.S. Department of Labor."

Even if you fail to include a COLA clause in your agreement, in some states, you can petition the courts for an automatic increase under a relatively easy process that doesn't require an attorney.

If you are the paying parent, you may be reluctant to include a COLA clause in your settlement agreement if one is not required by the laws of your state. But, there are definite advantages to you for including such an agreement. By including such a clause, you will be decreasing the odds that you will be dragged back into court by your ex-spouse requesting an increase of child support. That will save a great deal of money in attorney fees, not to mention aggravation. In addition, a COLA clause in your divorce decree will ensure that your children's financial needs are met as they grow.

Agreeing to an automatic cost of living increase does not lock you into future payments you cannot afford. If your circumstances change and you cannot afford the amount you've been paying—for example, you lose your job or become totally disabled—you can petition the court for a decrease. (See Smart Way number 57.)

INCLUDE LATE PAYMENT FEES

Whatever the amount of child support that has been negotiated or ordered, it is important that the support be paid in a timely fashion, so that the money will be available to meet the needs of your children.

If you receive support, try to include a clause in your final divorce settlement agreement that makes your ex-spouse liable for a late fee if he is delinquent in his payment of child support. This may motivate your ex-spouse to make timely payments that he might otherwise let slide in favor of paying bills that charge interest and late fees.

If you pay support, you may resist having a clause regarding late fees included in your divorce decree. But recognize that it is to your children's advantage to have the support they need. It is also to your advantage not to fall behind in support payments, as you don't want to pay legal costs (when you are hauled into court for failure to pay support) on top of accumulated arrears. If you don't intend to fall behind in child support, then it should not matter to you whether or not the agreement calls for late fees, as you will never have to pay them.

AUTOMATIC WAGE WITHHOLDING ORDERS

Here is another reason you may never have to pay a late fee. All states have laws authorizing judges to order that child support be paid through some form of automatic wage attachment, sometimes called wage assignment or wage withholding. The wage withholding requires the employer to deduct from the employee's wages enough money to cover the monthly child support, and to send that money directly to the child support recipient at the end of the month.

But wage withholding orders have their limitations and therefore a late payment fee provision could be important. If the payer loses his job, the wage withholding order will be ineffective. If he is self-employed, wage withholding is not possible. If he is employed in another state, the process of obtaining a wage withholding order is more cumbersome. See Smart Way number 56 for further discussion.

BE WISE ABOUT EXEMPTIONS
AND DEDUCTIONS

Exemptions and deductions are offsets you may be able to claim against your income on your tax return because of dependents and certain expenses incurred.

Exemptions. Either you or your ex-spouse can claim an exemption for each of your dependent children. Under the general rule, the children can be claimed as exemptions by the parent with physical custody. If the parents share physical custody, the exemption goes to the parent who had physical custody of the child for the most days of the year.

Parents can alter the general rule if the custodial parent signs IRS Form 8332, which the noncustodial parent must attach to his tax return. This form grants to the noncustodial parent an exemption for the children named in the form. By signing this form, the custodial spouse does not lose the right to claim child care credit or medical expenses for that child on her tax returns.

In general, giving the noncustodial parent the exemption will save income taxes if the noncustodial parent is in a higher tax bracket than the custodial parent. For example, if the custodial parent is in the 15% tax bracket and the noncustodial parent is in the 28% bracket, allocating the exemptions to the noncustodial parent will save more than $300 per child in taxes each year. High income parents may not realize any savings, however.

If the noncustodial parent earns over $111,800 a year, IRS rules reduce the amount of exemptions he can claim and all or part of the exemption may be lost.

If the parents agree that the noncustodial parent will claim the exemption, the custodial parent can use the exemption as a carrot to encourage the noncustodial parent to pay child support. Include a clause in the settlement agreement stating that the custodial parent will sign Form 8332 only if the noncustodial parent has paid child support on time all year. If the noncustodial parent plans to make timely payments of child support, he should not object to including such a clause in the agreement.

Child care credit. If you're working, looking for a job or attending school full-time, you may be able to claim a child care credit on your tax return for child care expenses. Child care expenses for children under age 13 are deductible by the parent with physical custody of the children. Child care expenses are *never* deductible by the parent who does not have physical custody of the children.

If the parent without physical custody of the children agrees to share child care expenses, he should not pay those expenses directly, as he will not be able to claim a tax deduction for the payment. Rather, he can increase his child support payments to funnel the custodial parent funds to pay for child care. The custodial parent can deduct the child care expenses, which would be non-deductible if paid directly by the noncustodial parent.

If the noncustodial parent wants a deduction for the payment, he could pay the additional funds to the custodial parent as alimony, which is generally tax deductible. Before you claim a deduction for alimony, be sure that the payments meet all the requirements for deductible alimony, as outlined in Smart Way number 16.

PART 4

SAVING TAX DOLLARS— DIVIDING PROPERTY AND FILING RETURNS

You have two relatively easy ways to accomplish a fair—emotionally and economically—division of the property you accumulated during your marriage:

- Each spouse takes what he or she wants, you compromise on the items you both want and either sell or give away the items neither of you wants. Divide the proceeds of the sale fairly and don't worry about the values of the items you are each keeping. Why try to achieve an exact 50-50 division of your property if you are getting what you want by dividing it otherwise?
- Total up the value of the property you own and divide it so that each spouse receives approximately 50% of the marital property.

In reality, most spouses go the first route. But many—especially those who turn their divorce over to a lawyer—go the second route. They generally come out of the marriage with approximately half of what was accumulated during the marriage, less the lawyer's fees it takes to get that property.

When going the second route, the challenge is valuing the marital property. The value of a piece of property is essentially its fair market value less the total amount of debts against it. For example, the value of your house is its fair market value (appraisal value) less the outstanding mortgage, home equity loan, tax liens and any other such debts. Although this sounds simple, it can be complex. In valuing your property for the purpose of dividing it, you may also want to consider income taxes due in the future.

In this section, we address the many income tax matters that affect divorcing people—the income tax basis of an asset, in particular the family home, how to file tax returns, what to do about tax refunds and balances due and how to protect yourself from prior tax liabilities.

DECIDE WHETHER TO FILE YOUR TAX RETURN SEPARATELY OR WITH YOUR SPOUSE

If you are still married on the last day of the year—that is, your divorce won't become final until the next calendar year—you have three options for filing your tax returns. You can file jointly, you can file as a married person filing separately or you can file as a head of household, if you qualify. When you are ready to file, calculate your liability jointly or separately to determine which is more advantageous.

It may make sense to delay filing your tax return (get an extension) to allow time for a full evaluation of the best way to file. To get an extension, you must file IRS Form 4868, Application for Automatic Extension of Time to File U.S. Individual Income Tax, by April 15. But you must pay the taxes due when you file the extension. When you later file your return, you can seek a refund of any overpayment.

The automatic extension lasts until August 15. If you are still not ready to file, complete IRS Form 2688, Application for Additional Extension of Time to File U.S. Individual Income Tax. You must file this by August 15 and state your "good cause" for needing more time for filing your return. This second extension is discretionary with the IRS. If it's granted, you have until October 15 to file your return.

If you decide to file jointly or have already filed a joint return, be sure you have a written agreement designating how you will share any refunds or taxes due on the joint tax return. Be sure to include this agreement in your settlement agreement.

If you file separately, you and your spouse can later amend and file jointly if doing so makes financial sense. The reverse is not true, however—once you file a joint return, you can not amend it to file separately. Smart Way number 30 contains more information on filing separate returns.

If You are in Doubt, File a Separate Return

You and your spouse can file joint income tax returns if you are still married at midnight on December 31. For couples still married on December 31, it is simpler to file a joint return than to file two separate tax returns. But in most states, there is an advantage to separate returns. The income for the year will be allocated to the person who earned it and filing a joint return means the spouse who had little income may pay more taxes than she would pay if the spouses filed separate returns.

For example, assume Sally earned $20,000 and had $6,000 federal income tax withheld. Harry's salary was $80,000, including his bonus, and his withholding was $17,000. Harry moved out on New Year's Day and sent Sally and their son support all year long. But there was no court order or written agreement, so the support he paid is not deductible by him nor is it taxable to Sally.

If Harry and Sally file jointly, they will owe $20,256 in federal taxes. Their combined withholding was $23,000, so they will receive a refund of $2,744. They agree to split it one-fifth to Sally ($549) and four-fifths to Harry ($2,195).

But if Sally and Harry file separately, Sally will be much better off. She is entitled to file as head of household because she supported her son more than half of the year. On $20,000 total income, she owes only $1,571 in federal taxes and would receive a refund of $4,429.

Harry, however, won't be in such good shape. As a married person filing separately, he owes a total of $19,761 in taxes. With only $17,000 withheld, he must pay the IRS an additional $2,761.

If Harry and Sally wanted to split the refunds and obligations equally (despite their unequal incomes), they would be much better off filing jointly. Then, they'd each be entitled to $1,372 ($2,744 halved). Filing separately, the net refund (Sally's refund less Harry's obligation) is only $1,668. Shared, it's only $834 a person.

If Harry and Sally live in a community property state other than California (Arizona, Idaho, Louisiana, Nevada, New Mexico, Texas, Washington, or Wisconsin), they report their income differently on their separate tax returns. In these community property states, all income earned during the marriage is shared equally until the date of the divorce—that is, Sally's $20,000 and

Harry's $80,000 would be reported as $50,000 for each (the taxes withheld would be split equally as well). This is not true in California, however, where income is shared equally only until the date of physical separation. And so in California, Sally would report $20,000 of income and Harry would report $80,000 of income.

If you are separated but not yet divorced, and you doubt your spouse's veracity in reporting income or deductions to the IRS, don't file a joint tax return. Both spouses are responsible for reporting all income on a joint return. If your spouse omits income, the IRS could—and probably would— come after you for payment. Protect yourself from paying taxes on income you know nothing about. Although you might owe more for the tax year in question if you file separately than if you file jointly, in the long run your filing separately could save you a bundle.

GET DIVORCED BY DECEMBER 31

For tax purposes, marital status is determined on the last day of the year. An attorney or financial advisor may recommend that you delay finalizing your divorce until January so you can file a joint tax return for the year prior to the divorce. But filing a joint return may cost more in taxes, not less, especially if you and your spouse have similar incomes.

Here is chart showing the federal income taxes for the filing statuses at various incomes.

Income of Each Spouse	Total Liability When		
	Married Spouses File Jointly	Divorced Former Spouses File as Single	Divorced Former Spouses File: One as Head of Household One as Single
$25,000	$5,910	$5,625	$5,355
$50,000	$19,910	$18,586	$17,074
$75,000	$35,317	$33,403	$31,483

UNDERSTAND THE CONCEPT OF TAX BASIS

The income tax basis of an asset or piece of property is how much you paid for it plus the cost of any improvements, minus the tax benefits you've received. Any asset or investment you purchase or receive as a gift, such as your house, stocks, bonds, mutual funds and rental property, has a tax basis.

The tax basis is important when you sell the asset. It is the amount you and the IRS use to calculate how much profit (gain) you made on the asset and therefore how much you owe in taxes. Bottom line, gain or loss is the difference remaining when you subtract what you put in (tax basis) from what you get out (sales price). If the number is positive, you have a gain and owe taxes. If the number is negative, you have a loss and don't owe taxes.

For example, you and your spouse bought 1,000 shares at $10 per share in XYZ mutual fund five years ago. It was a no-load fund (you paid no commission) and therefore the total amount you paid was $10,000. Assuming you received the dividends in cash (instead of reinvesting them in the mutual fund) and sold the shares at $15 per share or $15,000, you made $5,000. In this case your basis is $10,000 and your taxable gain is $5,000.

Another example of marital property that has a tax basis is your home. Suppose you purchased a home eight years ago for $100,000 and spent $20,000 on a new bathroom. At the time of the divorce you sell the house for $180,000. Your taxable gain is $60,000 ($180,000 sales price minus $100,000 purchase price and $20,000 improvements) less any sales commission and other costs of sale.

Knowing the tax basis of an asset is important—especially during divorce. The higher the tax basis relative to the item's current value, the lower the gain and taxes owed on that gain when you sell it. If you must choose between two assets of similar value during the divorce, you'll want to take the one with the higher tax basis so that your future income tax bill (when you sell) will be lower.

Suppose that you and your spouse own 1,000 shares in XYZ mutual fund and 1,000 shares in ABC mutual fund. Both are worth $15 per share, or $15,000. Your spouse says she doesn't care how you divide the funds—but she should. You bought ABC shares eight years ago at $5 per share and XYZ shares five years ago at $10 per share. Although both funds are now worth $15,000, each fund's taxable gain when sold is very different. On ABC, it is $10,000 ($15,000 minus the $5,000 you originally paid). On XYZ, it is only $5,000 ($15,000 minus the $10,000 you originally paid). The spouse who takes (and sells) ABC fund will owe much more in taxes than will the spouse who takes (and sells) XYZ fund.

DETERMINE THE TAX BASIS OF YOUR ASSETS

In Smart Way number 32, we explained the concept of tax basis. Be sure to read that if you haven't already done so, and then document the tax basis of all of your assets. When you divide property in divorce, with few exceptions, the property retains the tax basis it had when the two of you owned it. For example, you and your spouse bought a mutual fund three years ago for $8,000. The asset retains its $8,000 tax basis when you take it in the property division.

In knowing the tax basis, you can avoid taking assets with low basis (meaning assets that have gone up a lot in value) that will result in large tax liabilities when you sell them.

Here's how to find the tax basis of common assets.

Primary home
- Check the closing statement for total price paid, plus other costs paid at closing.
- Add any remodeling or improvement costs. Improvement costs are those that add to the value of the home, prolong its useful life or adapt it to new purposes. They include adding a bathroom or bedroom, putting in new plumbing or wiring, putting on a new roof or paving the driveway.

- Do not add the cost of repairs. These maintain but don't improve the property. Repairs include painting, fixing gutters or floors, repairing roof leaks and plastering or replacing broken windows.
- Deduct any untaxed gain from the sale of houses in the past. (This is explained below.)

Stocks, bonds, mutual funds
- See the "total amount paid" on the month-end statement or the statement that confirms buys which is sent to you by the brokerage house or mutual fund.
- Add any dividends you have reinvested.

Rental property
- Check the closing statement for total price paid, plus other costs paid at closing.
- Add any remodeling or improvement costs. Subtract any depreciation you've deducted on prior tax returns.

While the tax basis is the cost of the property plus any money you spent on improvements, in certain circumstances the basis can be less than this total number—meaning a higher tax bill. You can defer some or all of the gain on the sale of your primary house if you purchase a new house within two years of selling the old one.[5]

If you have deferred gains (you made a profit, but didn't pay taxes on the profit at that time) on the sale of homes in the past, the tax basis of your residence will be reduced by the untaxed gains on all previous houses you've owned. Although those gains were made while the two of you were married,

---

[5]Internal Revenue Code §1034

if you take the family residence in the divorce settlement, you will be stuck with paying all of the tax on the gains when you sell. You can defer paying taxes by reinvesting in a new home within two years that costs at least as much as the net sales price of the home you are selling.

For example, you and your spouse bought a home for $50,000 ten years ago. You added a bathroom and other remodeling in the amount of $40,000. You sold the home for $200,000 and paid a 6% commission, therefore netting $188,000. In this case, your tax basis is $90,000 (purchase price plus improvements) and your taxable gain is $98,000 ($188,000–$90,000). For the sake of simplicity, we are ignoring points, closing costs, and selling expenses including brokers' fees, fees for drafting the deed, escrow fees, title insurance, recording fees, title certificate and appraisal, all of which reduce your capital gain. If you then purchased a home for $225,000, your tax basis for that home will be only $127,000 ($225,000 less $98,000 of deferred gain). If you keep the family home after divorce, it comes with a low tax basis, despite its high original price.

Rental real estate may also present tax problems in addition to cash flow, tenant and maintenance headaches. Everything we've said about figuring tax basis and taxable gain apply to rental property, but there is an added wrinkle that complicates matters. Each year you are entitled to deduct depreciation from the amount of income the property generates; that accumulated depreciation reduces the property's tax basis and therefore increases the taxable gain when you sell the property. After a number of years, the accumulated depreciation will reduce the tax basis of the property to nothing but the original cost of the land, and virtually all of the net sales price will be taxable. In some cases, the taxes on that gain may exceed the cash you receive from the sale after the mortgages are paid.

KEEP TRACK OF LEGAL EXPENSES

Most legal fees and court costs for getting a divorce are personal and not deductible on your income tax return. But the Internal Revenue Code lets you deduct (as a miscellaneous expense on Schedule A) any money paid for advice related to the tax consequences of your divorce or for securing income. Deductible items include fees for advice on securing and collecting alimony, and the tax consequences of property and payments that you receive. Those fees may be paid to an attorney, accountant, mediator, financial advisor or other consultant.

A portion of the legal expenses that are not currently tax deductible may be added to the tax basis and become deductible when you sell assets you receive. Legal fees that you pay to negotiate the property settlement can be allocated among the assets you receive in proportion to their value. When you later sell those assets, you can then deduct the legal expenses from the sales price. You must be able to show that those fees were for time spent defending title to assets or obtaining them for you. For example, the cost of preparing and filing a deed to put title to a property in your name alone can be added to the tax basis of the property, and deducted when the property is sold.

Legal fees spent to increase alimony payments or to collect arrearages are deductible under the same theory. But that deductibility doesn't extend to the paying spouse. His legal costs attempting to reduce support payments or to defend against a claim for greater support are not deductible.

The rest of your legal expenses are not deductible, now or in the future. Non-deductible costs would include general divorce advice, counseling, advice and services concerning child-related issues, and any other fees or costs that cannot be directly allocated to one of the categories above.

Rather than having one spouse pay the other spouse's legal fees—in which case the paying spouse would not be able to deduct the payment—he would be better off paying additional alimony to cover the legal fees, which he can deduct. He can make the additional alimony payment directly to the other spouse's attorney, as long as the settlement agreement calls for payment to a third party. Be sure to review the alimony recapture provisions discussed in Smart Way number 17, however, before you agree to such an arrangement.

In order for you to claim a deduction for legal expenses incurred in a divorce, the attorney must make a reasonable allocation of the legal expenses between deductible and non-deductible advice. Ask your attorney to divide your bill into three parts:

- fees relating to tax advice and alimony that are currently deductible
- fees relating to property settlement
- fees that are non-deductible.

For the portion that is currently tax deductible, your attorney should append a certificate of counsel that states:

In the opinion of the undersigned, the amount of $X,XXX for legal services is deductible in the tax year in which paid under the provisions of Section 212 of the Internal Revenue Code as ordinary and necessary expenses incurred in connection with the production or collection of income, and in connection with determining and planning federal income taxation.

Any fees paid to a specialized professional, such as a tax attorney or certified public accountant, for tax and investment advice will be fully deductible even if it doesn't relate specifically to your property settlement. If you pay an accountant to help you determine the tax ramifications of your divorce decisions, the entire accountant's bill will be deductible as a miscellaneous deduction on Schedule A. Likewise, fees paid to a financial planner for advice concerning investments and financial goals will be deductible as a miscellaneous deduction on Schedule A.

There is one caveat in deducting attorneys' and others' fees as a miscellaneous deduction on Schedule A—they can be claimed only if your total miscellaneous deductions exceed 2% of your adjusted gross income.

WATCH OUT FOR PRIOR TAX LIABILITIES

If you believe your spouse may have omitted income or overstated deductions on prior joint tax returns filed by the two of you, make sure your settlement agreement includes an indemnification clause. In an indemnification clause, your spouse agrees to be responsible for any back taxes, and further agrees to repay you if the IRS collects those back taxes from you.

Even if your settlement agreement does not include an indemnification clause, you may not be liable for additional taxes if the IRS audits your joint tax return or bills you for undercalculating the taxes owed. Although both spouses are generally liable on all joint returns, if you can convince the IRS that you were an innocent spouse who knew nothing about the tax under-statement and did not benefit from it, the IRS may determine that you are not liable for the taxes due. Convincing the IRS that you are an innocent spouse is not an easy task. But if you qualify as an innocent spouse under the complex provisions of the Internal Revenue Code, you can fight the IRS assessment. If the amount is under $10,000, you can go to the small claims division of the tax court without a lawyer. For help, we suggest reading *Stand Up to the IRS*, by Frederick W. Daily (Nolo Press).

PART 5

UNDERSTANDING THE TAX CONSEQUENCES OF THE HOUSE

The family home is often the most valuable marital asset and most difficult hot button during divorce. A place of memories—children growing up, remodeling projects, gardening and happier times during the marriage—the home becomes a symbol of stability in an unstable time. One spouse, during settlement negotiations, usually fights for the home only to learn later that feelings won out over finances and that there are now tax gains and other costs associated with the house.

In this section, we explore options for the disposition of the home. Selling it now rather than later or selling it to your spouse may have some advantages you'll want to consider. If you and your spouse are both 55 or older, you can use special tax laws to exclude some or all of your capital gains if you sell the house.

SELL YOUR HOUSE NOW RATHER THAN LATER

If, in the near future, you plan to sell a house that has gone up in value, you might be better off selling it while you and your spouse are both owners. In general, when you sell a house, you will owe taxes on the capital gains unless you buy a new house of greater value within two years of selling the first house.

If you sell the house while you are both owners, you and your spouse will split the capital gains tax liability that results from the sale. If the house was the principal residence of both of you at the time of sale, you can each defer your share of the capital gains tax liability by purchasing a new principal residence that costs at least one-half the net sales price (sales price less all costs of sale) of the old residence. Although most people move on to more expensive houses, the opposite is often true after divorce. By selling your residence before you divorce, you probably won't owe capital gains tax on the sale even if you "move down."

If, on the other hand, you become the sole owner of the house in the divorce settlement, when you sell it, the entire capital gains liability will be yours alone. To defer the tax liability, you would have to buy a new home that costs at least as much as the entire net sales price of the old house. And this may be very hard to do after a divorce has reduced your financial resources.

Some couples agree to continue jointly owning the home after the divorce until a specified future time—for example, when the children are grown—and then sell the house and split the proceeds. But this can trigger a large tax bill for the out-of-house ex-spouse. Only one spouse (usually the custodial parent) will have had exclusive possession of the house until the sale. And under the tax law, only that ex-spouse can defer the capital gains by buying a second house after the sale of the first.[6] The out-of-house ex-spouse will have to pay taxes on his share of the net profit in the year of sale.

SELL YOUR HOUSE TO YOUR SPOUSE

Transactions between spouses during marriage or incident to divorce aren't taxable.[7] Therefore, if you sell your house to your spouse, you won't have to pay taxes on whatever profit your make. Nor will you be required to buy a new house within two years to defer the gain.

If you sell your share of the house to your spouse, you have a real advantage. You have cash to invest or make a down payment on a new house and you have no capital gains taxes to pay. Your spouse, of course, will have a tax liability when he or she sells the house, assuming it has appreciated in value.

---

[6]Internal Revenue Code §1034.

[7]Internal Revenue Code §1041

DETERMINING THE VALUE OF YOUR HOUSE

You can determine the value of a house in a number of ways.
- You can have the house appraised by an appraiser acceptable to both of you.
- If your house is similar to others in the neighborhood, you can ask a real estate agent to provide you with the price other homes have recently sold for and the listing prices of homes currently on the market. Also ask the agent to give you an opinion of your house's current value.
- You and your spouse can agree on a value that is acceptable to both of you.

If you recently bought or refinanced your home, don't rely on the value that the mortgage company's appraiser assigned to the house. Such appraisals are often low, to protect the bank and limit its losses in the event it has to foreclose.

If you plan to buy a new house after your divorce, thus deferring any gain, selling to your spouse may not be a major concern. But if you plan to rent, travel or not buy for any other reason, selling to your spouse may save a great deal in current taxes. If the value of your home is less than its tax basis (see Smart Way number 33), it will not matter when you sell your share of the house to your spouse or to another person, as there will be no gain.

IF YOU ARE OVER 55, DIVORCE BEFORE YOU SELL THE HOUSE

If you are a homeowner and over age 55, you may have a special tax advantage if your home has appreciated in value over the years. Under current law, an individual or a married couple can exclude from taxable income $125,000 of capital gain when selling a house. To be eligible, the individual or at least one spouse in the couple must:

- be 55 or older
- have owned and lived in the house as a primary residence for three of the last five years, and
- have not used the exclusion before because it is available only once.

If being able to exclude $125,000 of capital gain sounds good, how about $250,000? Although a married couple can claim only one $125,000 exclusion, you can claim $250,000 if you *each* meet the above requirements and finalize your divorce before you close escrow. After the divorce is final, transfer title of the house to you and your ex-spouse as tenants in common, which means that you each have a one-half interest in the property. When you sell the house, you can each exclude up to $125,000 of the capital gain. If your house total capital gain is less than $250,000 (including all gains deferred from earlier sales), you can exclude only up to the total amount of appreciation. You lose the amount unused.

Even if only one spouse is currently eligible to claim the $125,000 exclusion, you will still want to finalize your divorce before you sell the house. This is because if you and your spouse use the exemption during marriage (even if only one spouse qualified), the other spouse becomes "tainted" and can never use the exemption for himself or herself. If that spouse later marries, his or her new spouse becomes "tainted" and is unable to use the exemption as well. If you are divorced before selling the house, the non-qualifying ex-spouse will not lose the right to use the $125,000 exemption in the future.

If the divorce is final before the house is sold, and only one ex-spouse qualifies for the $125,000 exclusion, the other spouse will be fully taxed on her share of the gain unless she purchases a new house within two years of the sale.

PART 6

GETTING YOUR FAIR SHARE OF ASSETS

During your divorce, you will probably have little trouble identifying most of the property to divide, such as the family home, automobiles, and checking and savings accounts. This section discusses the less obvious assets, and some of the little-known benefits of obvious assets.

We help you plan your separation date, look for cash value in life insurance, document retirement plans, secure safe deposit keys, pay attention to bonuses your spouse might receive soon after separation, value any businesses or hobbies your spouse might have and calculate any interest you may have in your spouse's professional degree. We also point out the value in such things as frequent flyer miles, vacation days and pay, season tickets, club memberships, stock options and the like. Our goal is to help you receive your fair share of the assets.

PLAN YOUR SEPARATION DATE

Depending on the state in which you live, the decision of when to separate could have an impact on your share of property in the divorce. In states such as California, which exclude as marital property all assets received after separation, you'll want to stay in the relationship if you know your spouse is about to receive a bonus or pension plan contribution. Of course, if you are the spouse about to receive the money, you may want to separate in order to keep it all for yourself. (The spouse not receiving the money may argue that it was earned before separation and is therefore marital property. But meanwhile, the employee spouse will have had use and control of the money.)

In other states, such as New York, property received until the time the spouses sign a separation agreement or file the first divorce papers with the court is considered marital property. In these states, you may be able to physically separate sooner and not lose out on your share of your spouse's post-separation marital property. If you're the spouse about to receive the money, you might want to move quickly to prepare a separation agreement or to file the papers with the court before the money is received.

A ten-year marriage is considered to be a long-term marriage by the Social Security Administration. If you were married for ten years or longer, you will be eligible to collect Social Security benefits based on your ex-spouse's earnings record when you reach retirement age, assuming you are not married to someone else at the time. Those benefits are equal to one-half the amount your former spouse is eligible to collect, based on your spouse's earnings over his entire career, including the years after your marriage was dissolved. If you are divorcing a person with great future earnings potential and you've been married nearly ten years, consider sticking it out a little longer or delay finalizing the divorce until after the ten year mark.

Of course, if you have been employed for a number of years, Social Security benefits based on your own earnings record may be greater than the derivative benefits to which you might be entitled based on your former spouse's earnings. (You are not entitled to receive both.) In that case, you would collect benefits based on your own earnings record and there is no need to stretch out your marriage to be eligible for benefits derived from your spouse's work history.

TRACE SEPARATE PROPERTY

During your marriage, you probably have acquired property such as a house, retirement plan, stocks, bonds, cars and the like. If these assets were acquired with income received during the marriage, they are considered marital property and are part of the assets you will want to divide during divorce. On the other hand, if these assets were bought with money one of you brought into the marriage or with income generated from separately owned property, the asset bought during the marriage may be considered the separate property of the spouse with the income or income-producing property. In most states, it is separate property and not eligible to be divided during divorce.

If during your marriage you alone receive any gifts or inheritances or are paid for a personal injury you sustain, in many states these items or payments are considered your separate property even though you received them during marriage. You might have trouble tracing the specific funds, however, if you mix this money with marital property.

Sometimes, the property you and your spouse are dividing has both separate property and marital property components. This may be the case, for example, if you used an inheritance (separate property) as a down payment on a house and then used income from your job (marital property) to make the mortgage payments and to pay for improvements.

Each state has guidelines for determining whether property is characterized as separate, marital or a combination. For more information on this topic, we recommend *Divorce and Money: How to Make the Best Financial Decisions During Divorce*, by Violet Woodhouse and Victoria F. Collins, with M. C. Blakeman (Nolo Press).

The important point is this: To save money, you may need to obtain records that can help you trace separate property you believe should not be divided at divorce.

LOOK FOR CASH VALUE IN LIFE INSURANCE POLICIES

Review any whole life or universal life insurance policies you or your spouse might have to determine the cash value. If the policy was purchased or premiums paid during your marriage, the cash value may be considered marital property to be divided at divorce. This will be the case unless the policy was purchased and all premiums were paid with one spouse's separate property funds or by a business belonging to only one spouse. If the policy was paid for with community or marital property, however, the policy's cash value is marital property.

DOCUMENT RETIREMENT PLANS

Retirement plans are property to be divided at divorce, just as your house, cars and bank accounts are. In community property states (Arizona, California, Idaho, Louisiana, Nevada, New Mexico, Texas, Washington, and Wisconsin), only the portion of the retirement plans earned during marriage is subject to division. In most other states, a court would consider all retirement benefits in arriving at an equitable division of the marital property.

Retirement plans come in many different shapes and sizes. Individual Retirement Accounts (IRAs) are the most basic. IRAs are accounts you have established with a financial institution and to which you have made contributions. IRAs are easy to value—total up the amounts you've deposited plus all interest earned on the account. Most IRA custodians send you periodic statements showing the value of your account. Retirement plans generally referred to as employee thrift plans—such as 401(k) plans, 403(b) plans, tax savings annuities (TSAs) and employee savings plans—are valued the same way.

Retirement plans known as defined contribution profit-sharing plans, to which your employer makes contributions on your behalf, are valued the same way. But if you are not currently entitled to all of the money in your defined contribution plan, then you are not yet fully vested in the plan. This means that you currently own only part of the funds set aside for your benefit, and must continue working for the company to become fully vested—that is, to become entitled to 100% of the money in the plan.

Your employer may also provide a defined benefit plan, which promises you a monthly retirement benefit based on a combination of your highest annual earnings and the length of time you were employed by the company when you retire. This kind of plan will require an actuary to value it.

Gather all documents you have for all retirement plans owned by you and your spouse. Don't forget plans established through previous employers or set up before marriage but to which you contributed during the marriage.

You and your spouse have several ways in which you can deal with retirement plans. The simplest option is for you to keep the retirement plans and IRAs that are in your name and for your spouse to keep the plans in your spouse's name. If the amounts are considerably different, you can make up the difference in how you divide your other assets.

Another way to divide the retirement plan is for each of you to keep a portion of the plan (or plans). This is more complicated, as it requires something called a Qualified Domestic Relations Order (QDRO, pronounced quadro). A QDRO is a court order which must be served on (delivered to) the retirement plan administrator for the plan listed. Drafting a QDRO requires special knowledge and should be done by a domestic relations (or family law) attorney or a QDRO specialist.

The QDRO identifies the non-employee spouse (called the alternate payee) and identifies the alternate payee's interest in the plan. It specifies what the plan administrator is to do with that spouse's share of the plan. These are the options:

- Segregate the alternate payee's portion of the plan until the employee spouse reaches retirement age, then make monthly payments to the alternate payee.
- If the plan allows, distribute the full amount of the money due the alternate payee directly to an IRA owned by the alternate payee.

- Distribute the full amount of the money due the alternate payee directly to the alternate payee. The alternate payee can either keep the money and pay tax on it now, or roll it into an IRA within 60 days, thus delaying taxability until the funds are withdrawn at retirement. The pension plan administrator will withhold 20% for federal income tax from the distribution. The alternate payee will not owe a 10% early-distribution penalty when filing taxes even if the alternate payee is under $59\frac{1}{2}$.

If you are the alternate payee and are in a low tax bracket in the year you receive a full QDRO distribution, consider keeping a portion of the QDRO distribution and paying tax on that portion at your low rate, rather than rolling the full amount of the QDRO distribution into your IRA. To decide whether or not to do this, you will need to estimate your taxable income for the year of the distribution. If you are in a low tax bracket, you'd save tax dollars by keeping the amount of distribution that would be taxed at that bracket. A tax professional can advise you.

If you are the alternate payee and you plan to roll over the funds into an IRA, request that the distribution be made directly to your IRA by the pension plan administrator. If *you* (not your IRA) receive a distribution from a retirement plan, the pension plan administrator will withhold 20% of the proceeds for federal income taxes. You can avoid this through a direct rollover into your IRA.

You do not need a QDRO to transfer funds from your spouse's IRA to your own, or vice versa. If you receive a distribution from an IRA and do not roll it over within 60 days, however, you will owe income taxes on the distribution, plus a 10% premature distribution penalty if you are under $59\frac{1}{2}$.

Your Choices When Your Spouse Has a Retirement Plan

Deciding what to do about retirement assets isn't as complex as it might seem. Here are some pros and cons of the three choices you have regarding your spouse's plan—trade your interest in your spouse's retirement assets for something else, stay in the plan as an alternate payee, or request that the plan administrator give you your share now (current distribution). Note, however, that in some states or under some plans, you have limited choices—you must either trade your interest in the retirement plan for something else or stay in the plan as an alternate payee.

Trading Retirement Assets for Something Else—Pros

- You save money and time by not having to draft a QDRO.
- You eliminate future dealings with your spouse.
- By giving up your interest in your spouse's retirement plan, you may be able to keep an asset you really want, such as the house.
- If you kept an interest in the retirement plan, you would have to pay taxes on the distributions when you receive them in the future. By taking certain other assets now—such as an automobile or an item with a high tax basis and little appreciation—you will save tax dollars.

Trading Retirement Assets for Something Else—Cons

- By giving up your interest in your spouse's retirement plan, you may be jeopardizing your future retirement income.
- Retirement benefits are not taxed until you receive them, which may not be for many years. If you give up retirement benefits now, and later sell other assets to fund your retirement, you will owe the income tax on the sale of those assets in the year of the sale, reducing the investable money that you have left.

- If the retirement plan is a defined benefit plan, it will have to be valued in order to determine what amount of other assets would be an equitable offset. This means more expenses and additional delay.
- You and your spouse may not have enough other assets to equal up the division if your spouse keeps the entire retirement plan.

Staying in the Plan as Alternate Payee—Pros

- You will be assured of retirement income in the future.
- You will not have to value the plan today. If your spouse has a defined benefit plan, valuing it today in order to divide it today means making certain assumptions about the future—such as life expectancy, length of employment and future earnings. Those assumptions may prove to be very wrong, so staying in the plan may be the only way to ensure an economically fair division of the retirement plan.
- If your spouse is not yet vested and you are unsure whether or not vesting will occur, staying in the plan may be the only equitable method to divide the plan.
- If you stay in the plan, you will not have to make investment decisions. (The plan administrator makes them.) If you take a current distribution, you will have to decide what to do with the money.
- If the employee spouse will reach retirement age soon and you will begin drawing benefits then, staying in the plan as an alternate payee may be your simplest option because the plan includes a mechanism to make payments to you.
- If the plan is growing at an exceptional rate, you can benefit from the plan's investment expertise.
- If the plan has certain growth or cost of living increases that can't be duplicated in an IRA, such as benefits based on the highest three or five years' earnings, by staying in the plan you could benefit by receiving very high payouts when your ex-spouse retires.

Staying in the Plan as Alternate Payee—Cons

- When you begin receiving retirement benefits, a court may decide you no longer need alimony.
- The economic ties between you and your ex-spouse are not completely severed.
- You will not be able to control the investment decisions for your share of the retirement assets, as you can if you take a current distribution and roll the money into an IRA.
- If your ex-spouse takes early retirement or your ex-spouse's employer files for bankruptcy, you may lose some or all of the retirement benefits.
- Your share of the plan will not be available until your ex-spouse reaches retirement age, except in some plans if you demonstrate a hardship before that time. If your ex-spouse continues to work after becoming eligible to retire, you do not have to wait to get your share.[8]Once your ex-spouse reaches retirement age—even if your ex-spouse continues to work—you can begin to collect benefits. This law does not allow an ex-spouse to frustrate the other's ability to receive retirement benefits once the worker reaches retirement age.

Requesting Current Distribution—Pros

- If you take the distribution and roll it into an IRA, you can make your own investment decisions.
- If you need cash now—for security or living expenses—you can keep all or a portion of the distribution, although you'll have to pay current taxes on it.
- You may begin to tap money rolled into your IRA earlier than you would as an alternate employee in the plan. Although IRA distributions

---

[8]See the Retirement Equity Act of 1984.

before age 59^1/$_2$ are usually subject to a 10% penalty tax, there is an exception that lets you take payments from your IRA at any age without paying the penalty. To qualify, you must receive a monthly distribution based on your remaining lifetime, and those payments must continue until you are age 59^1/$_2$ (and for a minimum of five years). For example, you are 50 years old, have $60,000 in your IRA and the mortality tables say you will live another 30 years. Now assume your IRA investments earn 7% per year. You may begin receiving payments of $400 per month. If those payments continue until you are 59^1/$_2$, you will owe no penalty tax for the premature distributions.

• By taking a current distribution, you may be able to save your ex-spouse's heirs (who may be your children, for example) some money if your ex-spouse's retirement plan is worth a lot. The IRS imposes a 15% penalty on retirement plan distributions in excess of $150,000, and on accumulations in excess of $750,000 when a plan owner dies. If you take a current distribution, you may be able to reduce the plan so that it escapes those penalties in the future.

Requesting Current Distribution—Cons

• You will have to make your own investment decisions.
• Lump-sum distributions you receive from pension and profit-sharing plans at retirement age may qualify for favorable tax-averaging rules that reduce income taxes on the distributions. To qualify, you will have to remain an alternate payee under the plan until retirement age, rather than taking a current distribution or an IRA rollover.

Do an Inventory and Secure Access to Your Safe Deposit Box

An important aspect of saving money during divorce is to protect yourself from losing it.

If you and your spouse have a safe deposit box, you will want to know what is in it. If the box contains valuable assets, such as cash, jewelry, stock certificates, or important papers, secure access to the box, or at least photograph the contents so that you have a record of what is there.

If you know what is in the box and you have both keys to the box, then you have secured access to the box, and you do not have to worry that your spouse will remove valuable possessions or papers. If you and your spouse each have a key, then you each have access to the box and its contents. This is not a problem if there is nothing valuable in it, or if you don't think that your spouse will raid the box.

If you are afraid your spouse will raid the box, you have several options. First, visit the box and photograph, videotape or take an inventory of its contents. Bring along a person who can attest to the inventory. If you photograph or videotape the contents, place a copy of the day's newspaper in the box to prove that the picture wasn't taken at an earlier visit. You will then have a record of the contents of the box as of a certain date. Because each entry to the box must be recorded by the custodian, if your spouse subsequently visits the box and some of the contents are later missing, your photographs will clearly show the discrepancies.

Your second option is to remove the contents of the box yourself. Your spouse may allege that you have appropriated property that belonged to both of you, however, and your action will probably aggravate hard feelings between you. Other alternatives include asking your spouse for the other key, or giving both keys to the bank for safekeeping, so neither of you has access to the box.

If neither of these solutions is feasible, you can file papers with the court asking for a restraining order that prevents your spouse from having access to the box. If you do this, be sure to serve (deliver to) the safe deposit box custodian a copy of the restraining order. Consider this move carefully; getting a restraining order can be both expensive and confrontational.

In some states, restraining orders are automatically put in place when you file for divorce. If that is the case in your state, and you have filed for divorce, you need only serve the safe deposit box custodian with notice of the restraining order to prevent access to the box. Automatic restraining orders are generally reciprocal, however, so be aware that you will be restrained from access to the safe deposit box as well.

Pay Attention to Bonuses

Be aware of any bonuses your spouse receives in the first year after separation. Bonuses paid soon after separation were probably earned during the marriage. In that case, the bonus is probably considered marital or community property and you are likely to be entitled to a share of it.

Value Any Business Owned by You or Your Spouse

If you or your spouse own a business, that business will probably be a part of the property division. A business that was started during your marriage with joint funds will be considered marital property.

If the business was started with separate funds, or if the business was already in operation when you married, your situation is more complex. Although the rules vary, in most states a portion of the business will be considered a marital asset. The marital portion may be the amount of joint funds used to expand an existing business plus the appreciation attributed to that contribution. In addition, the efforts of the spouse who operated the business may have contributed to the growth of the business during the marriage, and thus may have created a marital asset. Each state is different, and you must look to the law in your state for guidance.

Once you determine the portion of the business that is marital property to be divided, you must determine its worth. This is best left to a competent appraiser who visits the place of business and has access to the records. You can review the records yourself to obtain a preliminary idea of the business' value. Start with a list of assets and liabilities for the business, which is called a balance sheet. The assets are generally listed at cost, so you may have to determine their actual value.

You may also need to add assets and liabilities not on the balance sheet. For example, if the business reports on a cash basis, accounts receivable from customers and accounts payable to suppliers may not be on the balance sheet. Other assets that might not be on the balance sheet include property that has been fully depreciated but still has value, and the value of customer lists, patents or valuable "know-how" developed internally. Work in progress, future contracts or residuals may also be omitted from the balance sheet, as may below-market leases which have value. If you have not been intimately involved in the business and do not have complete access to business records, you will probably have a hard time obtaining accurate information for these asset categories unless you subpoena documents and use other legal methods to obtain information.

Once you obtain sufficient information to adjust the assets and liabilities, subtract the liabilities from the assets to determine the tangible net worth of the business. Then add the value of goodwill, if any. Goodwill is generally value based on excess net earnings. To determine excess net earnings, deduct reasonable business expenses and reasonable salaries for owners from the gross income. Multiply the remaining amount by a factor between one and five (depending on a variety of factors, including the type of business, longevity, stability of earnings and earning trends) to determine the goodwill value of the business. The higher the net income and the higher the factor used, the greater will be the goodwill value.

If the income from the business is only enough to provide a living wage to the spouse operating the business, then the goodwill value is probably zero. Under the laws of many states, however, if the business could be sold for more than the tangible net worth of the business, the business will be assumed to have a goodwill value even if there are no excess net earnings. Your attorney or a business valuation expert can advise you on the law in your state.

DON'T OVERLOOK HOBBIES OR SIDE BUSINESSES

Don't overlook your spouse's hobbies or side businesses. For example, your spouse may enjoy weaving, marketing the handicrafts at fairs, craft shows and neighborhood shops. She may have looms, spindles, treadles and a wide array of finished work, dyes and yarns. The equipment and inventories are marital assets to be considered in a property settlement, and the business may be lucrative enough to have some goodwill value as well.

The same thing would be true of a weekend auto mechanic who repaired the neighbors' cars. The mechanic tools are valuable, and the weekend repair business may have goodwill value as well. In addition, the money earned from side businesses is money available to meet expenses for the parties and their children, and should not be ignored when computing the family's income to determine support.

Don't Ignore Professional Degrees and Licenses

If you have a PHT degree (Putting Honey Through), be sure to total up the costs you paid for your spouse to obtain an education. Depending on the laws of your state, you may have a right to be compensated for the cost of the education, the degree may be considered marital property, or you may be entitled to support based on the money paid out.

Some states treat professional degrees or professional licenses as property. In Michigan, for example, a court can treat a professional degree as marital property to be valued and divided. In New York, a court will treat a professional license, but not a college degree, as marital property. Courts in

Arkansas and Missouri value and divide degrees when no other way exists to equally divide the marital property.

In many other states, including Arizona, California, Florida, Indiana, Iowa, Kentucky, Maryland, Michigan, Mississippi, New Jersey, Ohio, Pennsylvania and Vermont, courts can reimburse the supporting spouse for costs of the supported spouse's education. Some states consider the degreed spouse's earning ability when setting alimony, but don't consider the degree as property or allow reimbursement of costs. Other states combine the methods in various ways.

Even if your state does not assign value to the educational costs you helped shoulder, to be fair, your spouse might be willing to pay education costs for you to upgrade your marketable skills now.

TABULATE OFTEN OVERLOOKED ASSETS

Frequent Flyer Points

When you list the assets you and your spouse own, don't forget frequent flyer points you have each accumulated. There are three ways to split these.

- Some frequent flyer programs allow spouses to transfer points between their accounts.

- Some programs allow free tickets to be issued in the name of someone other than the frequent flyer.
- The travel benefits that the points represent can be valued and the non-flyer spouse given other marital property to equalize. For example, 25,000 miles may be valued at $500, the cost of a coast-to-coast domestic flight. Obviously, this is subjective and may lead to arguments.

Vacation and Sick Pay

No, you can't take your spouse's vacation for him. In some states, however, the accumulated vacation days can be valued, based on your spouse's daily earnings. You can then take a corresponding amount of other marital property.

Season Tickets

You and your spouse may have season tickets to the ballpark, theater or symphony. If you have two season tickets, you probably do not want to split them, because you would end up sitting side by side at the event. Generally, the spouse who has the most interest in the activity will bargain with the other spouse to acquire his or her rights to the tickets. If both spouses want the tickets, you could draw straws, or perhaps use joint money to purchase another set of tickets of equal value, so that each of you can have a pair of tickets. You could agree to use the tickets in alternating years, but that is generally not satisfying to an avid fan who has spent years building priority on particular events.

Club Memberships

If you and your spouse belong to an athletic or country club for which you paid an initiation fee, and only one of you wants to continue the membership, you can value your membership at the price it currently costs to join. The spouse wanting the membership takes it and the other spouse takes other property of similar value. If both of you want to continue membership, many clubs will split memberships of divorcing spouses, usually for a nominal fee.

Stock Options

You or your spouse may have stock options. A stock option gives the holder the right to purchase shares of the employer's stock now or later, at a price already set. If the stock rises in value, you can buy it at the set price, which could be considerably below the trading price.

The stock option has a value. It is the difference between the current price of the stock and the set price at which it can be purchased. The option would have no value now if the option price is higher than the current price of the stock. But it would have value in the future if the price of the stock goes up.

You have two choices for including the option in your division of assets. One choice is to value the option, leave it with the spouse to whom the option is granted and give the other spouse an asset of similar value. A second choice—which may be fairer if the non-employee spouse thinks the stock will substantially rise in value in the future—is for the spouses to continue to hold the option together, then exercise the option jointly to buy some stock in the future.

Some state laws specify that if the rights to the option have not yet vested (that is, the employee spouse does not yet have the right to exercise the option to buy), then the stock option is not marital property and is not subject to division by the courts at divorce.

Timeshares

Many couples own timeshares in vacation property. Unfortunately, the current value of the timeshare may be less than was paid for it, and perhaps even less than you and your spouse still owe on it. In fact, neither of you may want it. If that is the case, you have a few options:

- one of you can take it at no cost
- you can continue to own it jointly
- you can try to sell it
- you can deed it back to the financing institution, or
- you can let the financing institution take it back in foreclosure.

Not all timeshares are financial disasters and one or both of you may want it. If only one of you wants it, then simply give the other spouse a similarly valued item in exchange. If you both want it, you can continue to own it jointly and each use it half the allotted time every year or alternate use of the property each year.

Magazine Subscriptions and Professional Dues

Prepaid magazine subscriptions, professional dues and the like are marital property. If you prepaid for several years, these items could have considerable value to add to the marital property to be divided.

Prepaid Insurance

Generally, insurance—be it life, disability or casualty—is prepaid in quarterly, semi-annual or annual premiums. You and your spouse may be covered personally under life and disability policies and your real estate and automobiles may be covered under casualty policies for which substantial premiums have been prepaid. Consider these prepayments when you are dividing your property. For example, you prepaid $1,000 for one year's coverage of car insurance and only three months have lapsed. This means that $750 of the premium is still prepaid. The spouse who gives up the car should be reimbursed $375, or half of the prepaid premiums.

PART 7

TAKING ACTION NOW
FOR BENEFITS LATER

Certain actions you take during your divorce or even before you separate can save you money or provide you benefits much later. These include stashing cash, providing for property taxes and insurance, accumulating records on the assets you keep, paying bills using joint funds before you go and closing joint accounts.

STASH CASH

No matter how you do it, divorce is costly. Costs include court filing fees, possible legal expenses, duplicate living expenses for the spouse who leaves the home, transportation between homes for the children, costs incurred to make yourself feel better—shopping sprees, therapy, a good meal out—and a myriad of other drains on your financial resources. Keep in mind that the money previously used to support one household must now stretch to support two.

If cash is available, set aside cash reserves to use during the first few months of separation. Otherwise, you may have to borrow or run up costly credit card debt to fund your needs for living expenses.

Naturally, when it comes time to divide assets, you will have to reveal the cash reserves you have set aside. If you fail to do so, and your ex-spouse later discovers that you had secret bank accounts or other assets, in most states your ex will be able to open up the divorce case for the purpose of dividing those newly discovered assets, even though you may have spent them long ago.

The cash that you set aside should be safe and readily accessible. You will probably want to deposit the money into a bank account or money market account that you set up in your own name, and on which you can draw at any time. Don't be tempted to place your cash reserves in time deposit accounts or other accounts which pay a higher interest rate but limit your access to the funds. Remember, the purpose of these funds is to give you cash for use in the difficult and expensive time of divorce—if the money earns some interest, so much the better, but earning interest is not your primary purpose in setting aside the funds.

The account into which you deposit the funds should be in your own name only, and should not be a joint account with your spouse. The money should be available to you for your needs. You may even want to open an account at a financial institution where your spouse does not bank, so that the bank doesn't accidentally confuse or mix the accounts.

To decide how much cash you need, compute the expenses that you may incur in connection with the separation and subsequent divorce. This can include security deposits and rental advances, duplicate household furnishings and appliances, attorney retainers, filing fees, and therapy and group counseling costs for you and your children. If you will ultimately receive child support or possibly alimony, you may also need cash reserves while you are waiting for your spouse to send money, or while you are waiting for a court date to set temporary support.

To amass the cash that you need, save as much as you can from each paycheck and other source of income that comes in. Cut back on your expenses where possible in order to stash cash. Unfortunately, those cutbacks in lifestyle may be permanent, as it is nearly impossible to support two households with the same income that supported one household. If you receive extra sums of money, such as a bonus, a tax refund, or income from overtime or an extra job, tuck away as much of that income as you can.

EXPLORE SOURCES OF CASH

As you prepare for or work through your divorce, you may find that you are not adequately prepared for the expense of divorce. Here are some sources of cash that might help you. Keep in mind that money you borrow has to be repaid (a friend or relative might forgive a loan, but don't count on it)—so consider how you will pay back any money you borrow before signing on the loan agreement dotted line.

While many of the following suggestions may present some problems when you are divorcing and dividing property and debts, they are worth considering and may be the only options for raising cash.

- Credit cards that provide cash advances may be a solution, albeit a costly one. The interest rate charged on credit cards is generally quite high. If your only option is to charge, it's time to radically change your lifestyle or you will go straight from divorce court to bankruptcy court.
- A low-cost or interest-free loan from a parent or other relative would be less costly than using credit cards. Carefully consider the emotional and interpersonal costs of borrowing from friends and relatives, however, before you ask for money or accept funds that have emotional strings attached.
- If you own a home, a home equity loan may be a possible source of funds. If you qualify, these loans can provide a generous line of credit on which you and your spouse can draw for future expenses, with low required monthly payments.

But a word of caution: if you plan to keep the house and give your spouse other assets in exchange (or a note for half of the house), you will owe the entire balance of the home equity loan, as it is a mortgage against the home.

- If you have a 401(k) or other employee thrift plan at work, check to see if it allows you to borrow from it. Many of these loans are at low interest rates, and don't have to be paid back for a number of years.

- Consider selling unwanted items to raise cash. Be sure you both agree to sell the property and that no restraining order bars you from doing so.

- You may be able to borrow from another kind of employer retirement plan, although many plans let you borrow only to pay for specific hardships. Check with your employer for the requirements of your plan.

- If you have borrowed money from a bank or finance company in the past (perhaps to buy a car) or have a good business relationship with your bank, you may be able to borrow funds on a personal loan. The interest on a personal loan might be high, however, so be sure you understand the full costs and repayment terms before you borrow.

- Taking money from an individual retirement plan is an option of last resort. If you withdraw money from an IRA before you are age $59\frac{1}{2}$, you will be liable for a 10% penalty along with regular income tax on the money you withdraw. That is quite expensive, and will leave you with far less in liquid funds than you anticipated.

- Drawing on another type of retirement plan will subject you to the same penalties if you are below the minimum age for withdrawal, unless the money is withdrawn pursuant to a Qualified Domestic

Relations Order. (See Smart Way number 42 for more information on Qualified Domestic Relations Orders.)

Although these sources of cash can provide the money you need to proceed with your divorce, be frugal in your use of them. In using these cash sources, you are mortgaging your future. Don't incur expensive debt that must be repaid later unless it is absolutely necessary, and then borrow only as much as you need. Slash expenses to the bone before you borrow. (See Smart Way number 60.) It isn't smart to borrow to continue a lifestyle you won't be able to maintain.

AGREE HOW EXPENSES WILL BE PAID AFTER SEPARATION

After you and your spouse have separated, but before you are divorced, you will need to come to an agreement on how expenses will be paid. Otherwise, you may find yourselves engaged in frequent legal squabbles as bills come due. These conflicts can drain you emotionally, impede progress toward finalizing your divorce, and be expensive as well.

Unless you are both self-supporting, with fairly equal incomes, one of you will probably pay more of the expenses, or will provide funds to the other with which to pay those expenses. In order for the spouse providing the excess funds to receive tax benefit, the payment to the other spouse should be characterized as alimony in a written agreement. (See Smart Way number 16.)

If you own your house, and your property taxes and insurance are not included in your monthly mortgage payment, make sure your temporary order or other agreement specifies who will pay those expenses. Too often, future property taxes and insurance premiums are overlooked by judges when making temporary orders. You might find yourself back in court, which is costly, or paying the bill and trying to get your spouse to reimburse you for half.

GET RECORDS ON ALL ASSETS

You will need complete records and documentation on the assets you receive as part of your divorce settlement, for two primary reasons:

- to calculate the tax basis so you can determine gain or loss for tax purposes in the event you sell the property (see Smart Ways number 32 and 33), and
- for resale value or warranty coverage while you hold that asset.

For example, get the purchase contract, warranty and service records on your car. Not only will these records be important in documenting the tax basis and resale value, but they also have important information concerning repairs. Having these records may help you cut future service costs and increase the car's resale value.

This same theory applies to other assets such as appliances or computers. Records and documentation are especially critical for more expensive assets such as homes, rental property and investments.

DEAL WITH YOUR MARITAL DEBTS

During your marriage, chances are you accumulated some property and some debts as well. The general rule is that debts incurred during the marriage are the obligation of both spouses. As you and your spouse negotiate your settlement, consider one of these options for dealing with the debts you incurred together:

- You can use joint funds, or sell property you jointly own to pay off your debts.
- You can divide your property and your debts equally and each of you will be responsible for repaying the debts assigned to you.
- One of you can agree to pay the bulk of the debts and in exchange, will receive a greater share of the marital property or increased alimony as an offset.

The first option is the safest, as it will extinguish the debt. The second and third options are risky—your ex-spouse may not pay the debts assigned to her. If you choose the second or third option, your agreement is between you and your ex-spouse only. Creditors can still look to you for repayment of marital debts even though your spouse agrees to pay the bills in your settlement agreement. The fact is, you could end up:

- paying bills you didn't expect to pay—after having given up property or alimony in exchange for your spouse paying the bills
- with a damaged credit rating, or
- having to sue your ex-spouse for reimbursement of the debts you paid.

The three options we give to deal with debts assume you have some marital property—but what if all you have is debt? Take a close look at your needs and how you can protect your own interests. You may have to borrow money to cover your divorce expenses. But if building debt is a way of life for your spouse, divorcing him or her may be the only way to protect yourself from future indebtedness and to salvage your financial sanity and security.

Don't Put Off Expenses

Debts incurred after separation (or after the spouses sign a separation agreement or file the divorce papers, in some states) are the responsibility of the spouse who incurred those expenses. If you delay necessary expenses until after separation, such as new tires for your car, you may end up paying for them yourself. One exception to the general rule is for family necessities. Even after separation, food, shelter, clothing, medical and dental care, childrens' expenses and the like are joint bills and the spouses share responsibility for them.

CLOSE JOINT ACCOUNTS

Just because a debt is incurred after separation doesn't mean you won't get stuck paying your spouse's bills if it was charged on a joint account or credit card. Creditors may still come after you if your spouse defaults on payment, and your only recourse may be to pay the bill and try to get reimbursed from your ex-spouse.

You will want to close any joint retail, gasoline, charge or credit card accounts so that you will not be responsible for your spouse's charges. Write to the creditors (the address is on back of the statements) and inform them that you and your spouse are divorcing. Request that they close the account and cancel all credit cards issued on that account. You will want to state that you will not be responsible for any charges made by your spouse after the date of your letter. Most creditors will handle this with no problem, but some may request that you pay off the balance before closing the account. If the account remains open, take control of all credit cards issued on the account so your spouse can't continue to charge.

ACCOUNTS YOU WILL WANT TO CLOSE

- Joint credit, charge, department store and gasoline card accounts
- Joint checking accounts
- Joint savings accounts
- Equity credit lines
- Brokerage accounts

PART 8

SAVING MONEY AFTER THE DIVORCE

You're close to the end of your divorce and you're looking ahead to a new life as a single person. There are actions you can take as you wrap up the paperwork to save money and build a secure financial future. In this section, we look at enforcing and modifying child support and alimony, reviewing your investments, investigating medical insurance options, knowing your tax filing status, deciding whether to buy or rent, saving on life insurance, finishing the divorce paperwork, protecting yourself from potential bankruptcy and funding an IRA with alimony.

COLLECT CHILD SUPPORT DUE YOU

If You Receive Child Support, You Should Know that . . .

Under the federal Family Support Act of 1988, child support orders initiated or modified after November 1, 1990 must include an immediate wage withholding order, unless it is waived by the parties.[9] Under the order, child support is deducted from the payer's paycheck and sent to the recipient.

Beginning in 1994, a wage withholding order is required for all new child support orders. On existing child support orders, a wage withholding goes into effect if the payer is one month or more behind in making payments.

Wage withholding orders cannot be used if the parent paying child support is self-employed. In addition, they are sometimes difficult to enforce against out-of-state parents, unless the parent's employer has a place of business within your state. If the payer is employed out-of-state, a law adopted by all states lets you register your child support order in the other state, and then serve the employer.[10]

Another option is to file a petition seeking enforcement with your local district attorney or child support enforcement office, which will forward the

---

[9] 42 U.S.C. § 666 and follows.

[10] Uniform Reciprocal Enforcement of Support Act (or Revised Uniform Reciprocal Enforcement Act).

claim to the state where the payer resides. The courts of that state will determine under their own laws whether support is owed, and then will issue a wage withholding order or seek collection another way. All of this takes time, and by the time the proper papers reach the state in which your ex-spouse works, he may be long gone.

Other Methods to Collect Child Support

When a wage withholding isn't available and your ex-spouse falls behind in child support, here are other methods to investigate:

- Contact your local child support enforcement unit (sometimes an arm of the district attorney's or state's attorney's office). The unit can receive and disburse support payments and act as prosecutor in the enforcement process. It will first try to use voluntary methods of persuasion to have your ex comply with the support obligations. If that fails, it may sue your ex.

- The child support enforcement unit can contact the IRS and state taxing authority to have your ex's income tax refunds intercepted. The unit can go after a portion of disability benefits and workers' compensation. In some states, the unit can tap into public and private employer pension and lottery winnings.

- If you can't currently collect, you can sue, obtain judgment for the past due child support and record a lien against any real property the payer owns. You will be paid when the payer sells or refinances the property. Once you have a judgment, a court can appoint a receiver to preserve property that can be used in the future to satisfy child support obligations. You can contact a sheriff or marshal to seize bank and other deposit accounts, and if your ex is self-employed, to collect receipts from customers as they come in.

If You Pay Child Support, You Should Know that . . .

Paying your child support obligation timely will be far less expensive than becoming enmeshed in the costly web of collection. In most cases, the support will simply be deducted from your paycheck through a wage withholding order. Even if the court does not immediately set up a wage withholding order, the court will probably take steps to have it put in place as soon as you fall behind.

Other Collection Information to Know

- Your obligation to pay delinquent support will not go away for a very long time. In most states, delinquent child support is collectible by the custodial parent or the state collection unit until your child reaches 18 or 21. Many states also allow the custodial parent or state collection unit to collect delinquent child support for a few years after the child reaches the age of majority.
- The court can add to the child support arrears all reasonable costs the custodial parent or state incurred in collecting the support, often including attorney fees. And many states provide for interest—and even penalties—on delinquent payments.
- If you disappear owing child support, the custodial parent can file a declaration to that effect with the court. The child support enforcement unit can make a parent locator search using federal and state agency information and will notify the court of your last known address and employer. Parent locator services generally have access to state utility connection records, motor vehicle records and tax and property records. If a statewide search is not fruitful, the court can refer the case to a federal parent locator service, which can search records at the Department of Health and Human Services, Social Security Administration, IRS and Department of Defense.

- In some states, if you are chronically delinquent in paying child support, you may be ordered by the court to deposit one year's child support payments into an account to secure future support payments, or to post a bond to secure payment.
- In many states, you can be denied a business license or driver's license or have a professional license revoked if you don't pay child support.
- Arrears in excess of $1,000 will be reported to credit bureaus. This could effect your ability to obtain a mortgage, car loan, credit card or other loan for many years.

MODIFY CHILD SUPPORT IF CIRCUMSTANCES CHANGE

Chances are you or your ex-spouse will seek a modification of child support sometime before your children are grown. That is because changing circumstances can wreak havoc on the most carefully negotiated child support arrangement. If one of you loses your job, has a reduction in hours worked, or becomes injured or disabled, a support payment that once seemed sufficient or not too hard to pay will rapidly become unreasonable. Or perhaps inflation has eaten away at the child support amount, or one parent receives a raise. In any of these circumstances, one parent will want to request a modification of the child support order as soon as possible.

Child support orders are not modified retroactively. A parent who cannot pay but delays seeking modification is saddling himself with a mounting debt of child support arrearages that may take years to repay. A parent who finds her support increasingly inadequate but who fails to seek modification will gradually move herself into poverty.

In order to modify child support, you generally must show a change in circumstance since the previous order. Changes that qualify include:

- An increase or decrease in the income received by either parent—such as more income from a new job or increased salary, or less income due to a loss of job, disability or retirement.
- New needs of the children—for example, tutoring, counseling expenses, participation in sports, private school, music lessons or medical problems.
- New child sharing arrangements—for instance, the child moves in with the noncustodial parent or a relative or a friend, the parents share custody or the percentage of time the child spends with each parent changes. (Some states do not take into account the percentage of time that children spend with each parent in computing child support— check the laws of your state.)
- New child support laws—in most states, the change in the child support law (the adoption of guidelines or a formula) constitutes a change in circumstance giving rise to a modification.

If circumstances have changed such that you need to seek a modification, you do not necessarily have to argue in court to get one. Compute the amount of the modification you need, then present your request to your ex-spouse and ask for the change. If you can reach an accord, you can write up an agreement and present it to the judge for a signature.

The judge will review the amount in your agreement by calculating support using the state's guidelines. If the amount you have agreed to deviates from the amount required by state law, the court may ask some questions. If the agreed upon amount is above the guideline, the court will probably ask the payer if he can truly afford that amount. If the agreed upon amount is below the guideline, the court might ask you to include a statement in your agreement that the children do not receive public assistance and are not likely to receive public assistance in the future.

If you cannot reach an agreement, the parent wanting the modification will have to decide if the modification is worth the financial and emotional drain of going through the court system. (Even if you go to court, the court might not change the amount. For example, in Alabama, unless the new amount is at least 10% more than the current order, the court will probably deny the modification.) And the parent opposing the modification must decide whether it is more cost-effective to fight the modification in court than try to find a middle ground and avoid an expensive legal battle.

In reality, fighting over child support in court these days is almost useless. Most judges apply a cut-and-dry, two-part process: (1) Here's the formula. (2) Here's the result.

If you're very rich and arguing over amounts in excess of the formula, the judge may lose patience with a parent who doesn't want to share his wealth with his children. But at the same time, the judge may lost patience with a custodial parent who demands too much and refuses to recognize the realities of the noncustodial parent's obligations.

ENFORCE AND MODIFY ALIMONY IF NECESSARY

After the divorce is final and you go your separate ways, you will still maintain a connection if one ex-spouse must pay alimony to the other. If your
divorce agreement calls for non-modifiable alimony to be paid for a set
period of time, and if the payer faithfully sends the check each month, your
involvement with the legal system (and each other) will be minimal. If,
however, the payer does not faithfully make payments, or your agreement
permits future modifications, you may find yourself navigating the legal
system once again after the divorce.

Enforcing Alimony

Under the Federal Child Support Enforcement Amendments of 1984, all
states can take fairly harsh action to enforce child support orders.[11] Most
states authorize the enforcement of alimony under this law as well, if the
payer owes both child support and alimony.

A wage withholding order is the easiest and most effective way to assure
that alimony payments will be made on time, and many states now provide
for an automatic wage withhold, unless it is waived by both parties. The
wage withhold requires the employer to deduct from the employee's wages
money owing for support, and to remit the amount withheld to the recipient

---

[11]42 U.S.C. 651 and following.

at the end of the month. Wage withholding orders can be an effective way of collecting future support as well as past due support, but they have their limitations.

If the payer is self-employed, a wage withhold is not possible. In addition, a wage withhold is sometimes difficult to enforce out of state, unless the payer's employer has a place of business within your state. If the payer is employed out-of-state, a law adopted by all states that lets you collect on an out-of-state child support order might be used to collect alimony.[12] These kinds of cases are difficult when trying to collect child support; they are even harder when trying to collect alimony.

If the alimony becomes past due, the recipient can take legal action to garnish income—that is, have a portion of the earnings or other funds of the payer seized and remitted to her. Once the court issues a writ of continuing garnishment, it can be served upon any holder of funds for the payer, such as an employer or bank.

A recipient who is owed alimony can also seek contempt charges against a non-payer, but even if she prevails, her victory may be a hollow one. Crowded jails may prevent the payer from being jailed. And being jailed may prevent him from working to get the money to pay the alimony.

A recipient owed past unpaid alimony can try to obtain a court judgment for the arrearages (amounts past due). Once she has a judgment, she can record a lien on property (the property can't be sold or transferred until she is paid), levy on bank accounts (she will receive any money in the account on the day the levy is received), and garnish the wages of the payer.

---

[12] Uniform Reciprocal Enforcement of Support Act (or Revised Uniform Reciprocal Enforcement of Support Act).

Modifying Alimony

If your divorce decree does not mention alimony, alimony probably can be awarded at a later date if the ex-spouse needing the alimony makes a sufficient case for alimony before a judge. If both spouses waived future alimony in the decree, then in general, a court will deny a future request for alimony. If your decree states a set amount of alimony which cannot be modified, then a court won't modify the amount.

But if your decree says that alimony is to be paid until further order of the court, either of you may seek modification based on changed circumstances. For example, if you are the payer and have lost your job or retired, you can request a reduction. You can make that same request if the recipient has obtained a job or promotion and needs less support.

If you receive support and your ex-spouse gets a large raise or inheritance after your divorce, most judges will deny your request for an alimony increase for two reasons:

- you have not demonstrated that *your* needs have changed, and
- alimony is generally limited to the lifestyle enjoyed by the couple during marriage.

If you pay alimony and become unable to make the payments called for in your divorce decree, seek modification of support immediately. Because courts rarely grant retroactive modifications, your ex-spouse can seek enforcement of the past due alimony. Your only defenses are that the support payment was not due or that you made the payment when it was due.

Terminating Alimony

In most states, alimony terminates by operation of law when the recipient dies or remarries. Many divorce decrees and a few state laws also provide that there is a presumption of a decreased need for alimony if the recipient cohabits with a person of the opposite sex. Your decree may also specify that alimony will cease on a certain date. Most states will not modify such an agreement, although the state may retain the authority to change such an agreement if the recipient might otherwise go on public assistance.

If your decree does not provide for a set termination date, then alimony will continue until further order of the court. The payer may seek a termination any time if he can show that the recipient no longer needs support or that he can no longer pay support. For example, support may cease if the recipient has become self-supporting through employment or inheritance, or if the payer is unable to pay because of a disability.

In short-term, moderate-length and even some long-term marriages, alimony will generally be ordered for a limited period of time, and will then cease. If the court orders support to cease, it may nonetheless retain jurisdiction over the issue. This means that if at any time in the future an ex-spouse needs support, she can petition the court for an order reinstating alimony.

REVIEW YOUR INVESTMENTS

Take the time to think about your financial future and your new goals and objectives. Do you want to go back to school, go back to work, change careers or retire? Will you need money to buy a car, a home, rent an apartment, take classes, buy clothes for a new job or pay off debt? Start by identifying your short-term and longer-term goals and then determine the amount needed to fulfill each goal and your timeline for doing so. With this information, you can review the investments such as stocks, bonds or mutual funds you received as part of the settlement. Determine if they are appropriate to help you reach your goals.

If you've not been active in making investments or need basic information, start by reading *Money Magazine, Kiplinger's Personal Finance Magazine, Worth,* or *Smart Money—The Wall Street Journal's Personal Finance Magazine.* For more detailed information, read *The Wall Street Journal* and *Barron's.* The personal finance or business section of your local newspaper is an interesting and worthwhile read as well. Consider enrolling in a course on personal finance or investing (or even the financial aspects of divorce if one is available) through the adult education department at your local community college.

Depending on what you have to invest and where you are considering investing it, you may also want to consult with a financial advisor, such as a financial planner, banker, insurance professional, stockbroker or accountant. You will want to ask the following questions:

- How has this investment performed over the time we've owned it?
- What was the purchase price and what is the potential gain or loss if I were to sell it now?
- If I need cash flow from this investment, will it provide that?
- If I do not need income now, but need growth or appreciation for my retirement, is this investment appropriate?
- If my situation is uncertain and I may need money for a home or car or move sometime soon, will this investment provide the liquidity I need?

Here are some very basic rules. If you need current income, you'll want to own bonds that pay interest, or stocks that pay dividends. If you are seeking long-term growth, consider stocks—both American and foreign. Liquid assets are best kept in savings accounts, money market accounts or short-term certificates of deposit. Mutual funds, which pool money from many investors, provide the advantages of diversification, professional management and record keeping of sales, purchases, gains and losses. If you are making your own investment decisions, no-load (you pay no commission or sales charge on purchase or sale) growth mutual funds are an ideal vehicle for the average investor. *Money Magazine, Forbes, Business Week* and other publications regularly publish lists of top performing mutual funds.

Cut Expenses

Remember the adage "Two can live as cheaply as one?" That is definitely not true if the two are divorcing. In divorce, the money that formerly operated one household now must run two, so cutting expenses is mandatory. Don't put off needed medical procedures, car repairs, home upkeep or credit card payments. Those deferrals will haunt you later, when you are less financially able to cope with them. Rather, reduce your other expenses, beginning now. Here are a few helpful ideas to make every dollar count.

- Shrink food costs by clipping coupons, buying on sale, purchasing generic brands and buying in bulk.
- Improve your gas mileage by tuning up your car, checking the air in the tires and driving less—carpool and combine trips instead.
- Conserve water and electricity.
- Make long distance calls only when necessary and at off-peak savings rates.

- Spend less on gifts and vacations.
- Carry your lunch to work.
- Buy secondhand furniture and appliances.

INVESTIGATE MEDICAL INSURANCE OPTIONS

Under the Consolidated Omnibus Reconciliation Act of 1986, popularly known as COBRA, employers who maintain health care plans for 20 or more employees must offer identical coverage to ex-spouses and other qualified beneficiaries for three years after divorce or legal separation. The coverage is available only if group health plan coverage was in effect for the employee at the time of divorce or legal separation, however. For example, if your spouse works part-time and is not covered under the employer health plan, continuing coverage will not be available to you after divorce. Likewise, if the employer plan covers fewer than 20 employees, the ex-spouse may not be eligible for continuing coverage even if the spouse's insurance was in effect at the time of divorce.

If you plan to request COBRA coverage under your ex-spouse's plan, be sure that you are fully covered under the plan and have not waived coverage prior to the divorce. For example, you may have opted not to be covered as a dependent under your spouse's plan because you were covered under your own employer's plan. If you wish to be covered under your ex-spouse's plan, prior to divorce or legal separation your spouse must notify her employer that she wishes to reinstate dependent coverage. There may be a waiting period before the coverage can resume.

If you have a choice of coverage under the plan, such as private doctors or a group plan such as a health maintenance organization (HMO), the non-employee ex-spouse is entitled to make his own choice, regardless of the election made by the employed ex-spouse. The non-employee ex-spouse must pay for the coverage, of course, at a rate not to exceed 102% of the plan's cost for similar employees.

Generally, payments already made toward deductible and co-insurance limits will carry over into the continuation period. In the case of family deductibles, each family unit will have to satisfy the remaining deductibles.

COBRA coverage may terminate if the employer ceases to maintain health care coverage for its employees, if the ex-spouse fails to make timely premium payments, becomes covered under another group plan or becomes entitled to Medicare benefits.

If the employer modifies coverage for its employees, the modification will also apply to people included under the COBRA coverage continuation provisions. If the employer plan provides for a conversion privilege to an individual plan when employment ceases, that conversion privilege must be extended to the ex-spouse after the three years of COBRA continuation coverage expires. If the plan allow employees to add a spouse or dependent to coverage, the ex-spouse may also add a spouse or dependent.

If you are the employed spouse and agree to fund the health care coverage for your ex-spouse for a period of time, you cannot deduct the cost of your ex-spouse's medical insurance premiums and other medical expenses as a medical expense on your tax return because your ex-spouse is not your dependent. If your divorce decree requires you to make those payments, you may claim a deduction for them as alimony paid. Alternatively, you can increase your alimony payment required under your divorce decree, take a tax deduction and let your ex-spouse pay his own premiums.

Investigate all your options, and find out whether COBRA coverage is less costly than other plans available to you. If you opt for COBRA, at the end of three years you will either need to convert coverage to your own plan with the same company (which is likely to be considerably more expensive than the COBRA coverage) or to switch your insurance to another company.

If you have a pre-existing condition, you may not qualify for insurance at the end of the COBRA coverage. If you do qualify, the coverage is likely to not cover pre-existing conditions for the first two years you are insured. To ensure continuing coverage, consider taking out private insurance with a two-year exclusion period for your pre-existing condition within one year of beginning COBRA coverage. You will have COBRA coverage for your pre-existing illness for the three years. And the two-year exclusion period will expire just as the COBRA coverage expires, leaving you fully insured under your private insurance. This is expensive, however, and you will probably want to consider it only if you cannot get a job with full coverage at a reasonable cost.

If you are healthy, consider a private plan rather than taking the COBRA coverage for three years. If you took the COBRA coverage and became ill during the three-year period, you might find that you were uninsurable at the end of three years, when the COBRA coverage expired. A private plan, rather than a group plan under COBRA, would facilitate continuing coverage and might be worth any extra expense. And often, for young, healthy individuals, private plans are less costly than the premiums charged for the COBRA coverage.

To search for an individual hospitalization policy and major medical plan, consider the following sources: Blue Cross and Blue Shield, other preferred provider organizations (PPOs), health maintenance organizations (HMOs), other insurance companies, Medicare Part B and Medicare supplemental policies (if you are over 65) and group plans through professional societies and fraternal organizations of which you are a member.

When comparing policies and coverage, look for a high upper limit that covers at least $1 million of medical expenses before it stops paying. Then compare initial deductibles and co-insurance clauses, to determine what portion of routine medical expenses you would end up paying. Finally, note the kinds of expenses that are excluded or limited, such as dental costs, prescription drugs, psychotherapy, pregnancy, alternative practitioners (chiropractors or acupuncturists), cosmetic surgery and whatever else is important to you.

KNOW YOUR FILING STATUS

There are four basic ways you can file your tax returns depending on the stage of the divorce process you are in:

- Single—You have a court order of divorce or separate maintenance and you do not qualify for another filing status. If you were considered married for part of the year and lived in a community property state (Arizona, California, Idaho, Louisiana, Nevada, New Mexico, Texas, Washington and Wisconsin), read IRS Publication 555 describing special rules that may apply in determining your income and expenses.

- Married filing jointly—You can file jointly if you are still married and living apart, but do not have a court order of divorce or separate maintenance. You both must agree to file jointly and in doing so, you'll report your combined income and deduct your combined allowable expenses.
- Married filing separately—You are still married and may be living apart, but do not have a court order of divorce or separate mainte-nance. You may file a separate return reporting only your income and deducting only your expenses. You may pay more in taxes by filing this way, but it may be worth it if you question your spouse's integrity in filing tax returns. Also, if you file separately, you can always amend returns within three years to file jointly. But if you file jointly you cannot later amend returns to file separately.
- Head of household—You can file as head of household even though you are not divorced or legally separated if you live apart and meet certain tests. You can also file as head of household after your divorce is final. You may qualify as head of household if you:
  - ✓ file a separate return
  - ✓ paid more thxan half the cost of maintaining your home for the tax year
  - ✓ did not live with your spouse in your home during the last six months of the tax year, and
  - ✓ lived in your home which was, for more than half the year, the main home of your child, stepchild, or adopted child whom you could claim as a dependent, even if you did not claim your child as a dependent because you state in writing that the noncustodial parent may claim an exemption for the child or the noncustodial parent provides at least $600 support for the child and claims an exemption for the child under a pre-1985 agreement.

If you qualify and file as head of household instead of single or as married filing separately, your standard deduction will be higher. In addition, your tax rates will be lower than the rates for single or married filing separately and you may be able to claim the earned income credit.

You cannot file under one status for part of the year and under another for the remainder of the year. Your filing status for the entire year is determined by whether you are married or divorced on December 31.

GET THE CREDIT DUE YOU

As a single person, you have the right to obtain credit, and a credit report, in your own name. You can obtain a copy of your credit report from one of the "Big 3" credit bureaus—TRW at 800-392-1122, Trans Union at 800-851-2674 or Equifax at 800-443-9342. TRW will give you one free copy of your credit report each year; the other companies will charge you between $2 and $15.

If you find any errors in your report, return the dispute form enclosed with your credit report. The credit bureau must attempt to verify the information you dispute. If it can't within 30 days, it must remove the information from your credit report.

Be aware that joint accounts from your marriage are permitted to be in your credit report, even if your spouse agreed to pay those accounts as part of the divorce. Just because you divide the debts with your spouse does not change your original agreement with your creditors—you are both still obligated on the account—and the creditors can seek payment from either of you. If your spouse agrees to pay a joint account but falls delinquent, that delinquency may appear on your credit report.

If debts are a real problem for you during or after divorce and you need help, consider calling Consumer Credit Counseling Service. CCCS is a national nonprofit organization with offices in every state. For a nominal fee (which is often waived) CCCS can help you create a budget. If you have enough monthly income, CCCS will set up a repayment plan for you under which you make one payment to CCCS each month and CCCS sends money on to your creditors.

Each CCCS office is funded by major creditors, such as banks and department stores by retaining a small percentage of the money you pay them. CCCS does have clout to get late fees, over-limit-fees, other nuisance fees and some interest charges waived. CCCS may not recommend bankruptcy—even if it's appropriate for you—because in bankruptcy, the creditors who fund them may not get paid. Nevertheless, most people find CCCS very helpful. You can find the office nearest you by calling 800-388-2227. Under no circumstances should you use a for-profit credit "repair" organization or company that demands a large up-front payment. They can't do anything for you that you can't do for yourself, for considerably less cost.

For more information on credit reports, debts and re-establishing your credit, see *Money Troubles: Legal Strategies to Cope With Your Debts* or *Nolo's Law Form Kit: Rebuild Your Credit*, both written by Robin Leonard and both published by Nolo Press.

CONSIDER BANKRUPTCY

Money problems often contribute to marriage problems, and vice versa, so it is not unusual for people contemplating divorce to be contemplating bankruptcy at the same time.

Personal bankruptcy allows you to delay paying your bills, or to escape payment altogether. In Chapter 7 bankruptcy, your debts are forgiven, or discharged. In exchange, you may have to give up some of your assets, although very few people lose any property in Chapter 7 bankruptcy. Some debts cannot be discharged, however, such as most taxes, alimony and child support, traffic tickets and criminal fines, and student loans where payments have first become due within the past seven years.

Chapter 13 bankruptcy lets individuals repay a portion of their debts over three to five years, in periodic installments. The rest of your debts are forgiven. Chapter 11 bankruptcy lets any business or an individual with very high debts reorganize their finances.

If bankruptcy seems to be the best answer for your debt burden, and you haven't yet divorced, you must decide whether to divorce or go bankrupt first. In general, if both spouses are considering bankruptcy—and they probably should be if they are both liable for all the debts—filing separately after divorce will cost more in filing fees and attorney's fees (if you use a lawyer).

It may also be fairer to both spouses if the bankruptcy comes before the assets and debts are split in divorce. For example, assume that your primary asset is your marital home, and you also have a great deal of debt. If your spouse agrees to assume most debts in exchange for keeping the house, you will end up with very little in the property settlement. If your ex-spouse declares bankruptcy after the divorce, the debt will be discharged, and your ex-spouse may be allowed to keep most or all of the equity in the home. Now, you have nothing and your ex-spouse has the house, so the relative solvency of the spouses would be greatly skewed.

PROTECT YOURSELF AGAINST BANKRUPTCY AFTER DIVORCE

Here's a scenario even worse than the one just described above. Again, assume that your primary asset is your marital home, and you also have a great deal of debt. This time, your spouse takes the house and the debts, but you are entitled to something. So your spouse gives you a note for your share of the equity, secured by the house. When your ex-spouse declares bankruptcy after the divorce, the debts—including quite possibly the note due you—will be discharged, and your ex-spouse will probably be allowed to keep most or all of the equity in the home. It often takes very careful wording and drafting of a note to avoid it being wiped out in bankruptcy.

There is one good bit of news—if your ex-spouse files for bankruptcy after your divorce, he cannot discharge any alimony or child support owed to you under a separation agreement, divorce decree or court order or property settlement, except in the following situations:

- Support owed under a state's general support law, not a court order. If your ex-spouse is paying you under the general law of your state that requires parents to support their children, or spouses to support each other, and no court actually ordered the support, the debt is dischargeable.

- Support owed someone other than a spouse, ex-spouse or child (except the welfare department). If a former or current spouse or a child has given (assigned, in legal terms) the right to receive the support to someone else, or a creditor has garnished the payments, the debt is dischargeable.

A court order setting the amount of child support payments is clear enough to prevent discharge in bankruptcy. Some other debts, however, may also be considered non-dischargeable child support or alimony. The most common are marital debts—the debts a spouse was ordered to pay when the couple divorced.

Often, the spouse who's paying alimony or child support agreed at the time of the divorce to pay more than half of the marital debts. If that spouse later files for bankruptcy, the bankruptcy court might rule that a portion of the debt is really support. Consequently, it's considered a non-dischargeable debt owed to the other spouse. Similarly, one spouse may have agreed to pay some of the other spouse's or children's future living expenses (shelter, clothing, health insurance, transportation). Again, the bankruptcy court may very well treat the obligations for the future expenses as support owed to the other spouse and not allow them to be discharged.

Obligations that are generally considered support and aren't dischargeable include debts that:

- are paid to a spouse who is maintaining the primary residence of the children while there is a serious imbalance of incomes
- terminate on the death or remarriage of the recipient spouse
- depend on the future income of either spouse, or
- are paid in installments over a substantial period of time.

For a Home Base—Consider Renting Versus Buying

Until you are sure of your finances and where you want to live in the future, rent rather than buy. Closing costs, financing points and other expenses make home purchase a costly proposition. If you and your spouse have sold your former home, you will have two years from the date of that sale to reinvest in a new home and defer the gain. (See Smart Way number 36.) Although you want to anchor yourself emotionally after divorce, rushing to purchase a new home may not anchor you—it may sink your ship. Slow down and get settled into your new life before you make important decisions such as buying a home.

As time passes, you will become more clear on where you want to live and work, and the financial obligations you'll have to meet. If you find you have the necessary down payment for a house and a capital gains liability to defer, you'll still want to consider the pros and cons of buying versus renting.

Answer these five questions and you'll have a good basis for making your decision.

- How much can you save each year by paying rent rather than mortgage payments? To compute mortgage payments, figure the amount you would finance after making a down payment, then consult an amortization table at your library or use a financial calculator to figure the mortgage payment for a 30-year loan at today's interest rates. Multiply the mortgage payment by 12 to get the annual total, then add to that amount the insurance and property taxes, and the monthly homeowner association fees, if any, multiplied by 12. If you are flush with cash, have a good monthly income and want to pay off your mortgage quickly to save interest, check into a 15- or 20-year loan. The monthly payments will be higher than one amortized over 30 years, but you'll save an enormous amount by paying less interest.

- How much can you save each year in income taxes by buying a home rather than renting? To compute your home mortgage interest deduction, multiply the loan amount by the interest rate. Add to this amount the annual property taxes and multiply the total by your tax rate (consult the tax rate schedules that came with your federal and state tax return forms).

- If you sold your former residence, how much will you owe in capital gains tax if you don't defer the gain (see Smart Way number 36)? Compute the amount by multiplying your share of the net gain on the sale (see IRS Form 2119 of your income tax return for the year of sale) by your tax rate for the year (see the tax rate schedules that accompanied your federal and state income tax return forms).

- If you didn't purchase a new home, how much would you earn if you invested the money available for a down payment, after paying the income taxes on the sale of your prior residence? Multiply the available down payment, less the income taxes computed above, by the rate you might earn on an alternate investment. The earnings rate will probably range from the current interest rate on certificates of deposit, if you are an ultra-conservative investor, to an average growth and earnings rate of 10% or so if you invest in stocks or equity mutual funds, or perhaps a blended rate of 7% to 10% if you invest in a diversified mixture of cash instruments, stocks and bonds.

• How much can you expect the new home to increase in value each year? Although no one has a crystal ball to predict house appreciation, you may want to attempt to compute an amount. Consult several realtors and bankers to arrive at a consensus of opinion on the anticipated appreciation rate. (If the general opinion is that property in your area is declining, this may be a negative rate rather than a positive one.) Multiply the current market value of the new home by your estimate of the appreciation (or the declining value) rate.

Be aware that the consensus of opinion may not be right. Just because property values have gone up in the past, that is no indication that they will appreciate in the future. Real estate professionals sometimes exhibit unwarranted optimism about real estate's future value. In making your calculations, it is best to be pessimistic and assume no appreciation, or a possible loss in value.

Use the following worksheet to compare the options of renting or buying. Fill in the amounts you computed, above.

	Column 1 Renting	Column 2 Buying
Savings of renting over buying	_____	
Tax savings of buying		_____
Anticipated annual appreciation (or loss in value)		_____
Capital gains taxes due		_____
Lost earnings on down payment	_____	
Total	_____	_____

If the sum of column one is greater than the sum of column two, the money you would save by renting is greater than the net benefits of buying. Thus, consider renting until you anticipate conditions might change—for example, until rents go up, income taxes increase, investment earnings rates decrease. But if you plan to stay in a house for a long time, the advantages of a fixed-rate mortgage may outweigh any savings in rents, because rents generally go up over the years, while a fixed-rate mortgage payment would stay the same. Thus the advantage of renting over buying could evaporate in just a few years.

If sum of column two is greater than sum of column one, the combined net benefits of buying are greater than the money you would save by renting. Check your assumptions and computations one more time. If the figures still hold, you will probably find it to your benefit to buy rather than to rent.

But a word of caution: If you plan to sell your new house in two years or less, you should consider renting rather than buying. In most markets, the increase in value of your residence for the first two years will be consumed by the cost of selling the residence—commissions, title insurance, closing costs and the like. If you sell within a year or two, the appreciation in your home may be little, if anything. You may even lose money if the net sales price, after commissions and expenses, is less than your original cost of the property. In general, real estate is not expected to appreciate in the future as it has in the past, so don't make your decisions on outdated assumptions.

SAVE ON LIFE INSURANCE

Even after divorce, life insurance may be necessary. This is especially true if you have young children or other dependents such as parents or other relatives who depend on you for support. If you are receiving child support or alimony, you will probably want to insure your income stream (also known as your ex-spouse) if there are funds left after paying for rent, food, clothing and your other basic expenses. Be sure you are named as beneficiary on any life insurance policy owned by your ex-spouse for as long as he is required to pay you support.

If you need life insurance, should you buy term or whole life insurance to insure yourself and/or your ex-spouse? Term policy premiums are less expensive than whole, but have no cash build-up. Whole life policies, including universal life, are more expensive than term, but have cash value building up within the policy. Whole life may be viewed as insurance coverage plus an investment component. It helps to think of the renting versus owning your home analogy. Term insurance is like renting: you have nothing to show at the end of each year. Whole life is like owning: you have equity growing in your investment over the years.

One strategy you might consider to save money and build assets over time is to buy term insurance and invest the premium difference in an investment outside of the insurance policy, such as tax-free municipal bonds. If the term policy costs $400 and the whole life policy $1,400, what rate of return can you expect on that $1,000 difference? If the alternate investment has a higher (or equivalent) return and fewer restrictions, the answer is obvious.

To determine which term policies are most cost-effective, check with a free rate-shopping service such as Select Quote at 800-343-1985, Insurance Quote at 800-972-1104 or Term Quote at 800-444-8376. These groups make money if you buy a product they recommend, so use the information you get only as your starting point. Check also for no-load whole life policies, where you pay no sales charge or commission. These are offered through fee-only (no commission) agents or financial planners or can be purchased directly through the insurer.

GET A COPY OF YOUR FINAL DECREE

When your divorce is final, be sure to obtain a court-certified copy of the decree for your files. You will need it in the future for a number of reasons.

- It is proof that you are actually divorced, and you will need it for authorities such as the Social Security Administration.
- If you later seek modification of the support provisions of your decree, such as child support or alimony, you will need a copy of the decree to show the attorney, if you use one.
- If you bring a subsequent action for modification or enforcement of support in a court other than the one in which you were granted your divorce, you will probably need to file a copy of the decree with the new court.
- If you seek a wage withholding order from your spouse's new employer, you will need a copy of the decree to prove the amount of support which is required to be withheld.
- To enforce child support through the child support collection unit, you will need a copy of the final decree to show the amount of support.
- To enforce support in another state, you will need a copy of the final decree to file as an out-of-state order with the state in which you seek to have support orders enforced.

- If you apply for a loan and pay or receive support, you may be asked to provide a copy of the final decree to prove the amount of support you pay or receive.
- If you are granted sole ownership of your residence or other real property, your mortgage company may require a copy of the final decree to transfer the mortgage to your name.
- Your accountant or lawyer may want to see a copy of the final settlement agreement when preparing future tax returns or drafting new wills or trusts for you.

CHANGE BENEFICIARY DESIGNATIONS

Rewrite your will to ensure that your new intentions regarding inheritance are reflected. Be sure to also change beneficiary designations where necessary for retirement plans, IRAs, life insurance and any other assets payable in beneficiary form.

FUND AN **IRA** WITH ALIMONY

If you're not earning an income but will receive alimony, you can fund an Individual Retirement Account for up to $2,000 a year (assuming that your alimony equals or exceeds $2,000 a year) if you are not covered under an employer retirement plan or your income is under $25,000 a year. The advantage of an IRA is that interest and appreciation on the account are tax-deferred so you pay no taxes on the growth in the account until you begin to withdraw money at age 59½ or later. If you are in the 31% federal income tax bracket, your tax savings from contributing to an IRA is $620 per year. If your state has an income tax, your savings from an IRA deduction will be even greater.

Appendix A

Sources of Taxable Income

- Agreement not to compete payments
- Airline deregulation unemployment benefits
- Alimony payments received
- Annuity payments in excess of the cost of the annuity
- Annuity interest earned on premiums paid in advance
- Award and prizes from any source
- Back pay
- Bonuses
- Buried treasure and treasure trove
- Checks you wrote for previously deducted items that were never cashed
- Clergy pay contributions and other compensation
- Commodity credit loans received may be reported either in the year received or the year the commodity is sold.
- Compensation paid in property received
- Contest winnings
- Contract or lease cancellation payments
- Damages for loss of anticipated business benefits
- Death benefits from employer's plan to which employee contributed nothing
- Debt cancellation or discharge
- Defamation damage award which compensates for injury to business and professional reputation

- Disaster unemployment payments
- Dividends in form of stock, distributed in lieu of money
- Drawing or advance account canceled by employer
- Employee discounts that exceed the employee's gross profit percentage
- Employment contract cancellation compensation
- Evangelist contributions collected
- Farm government payments to offset losses
- Financial counseling fees paid by employer
- Future services prepayments
- Gains from condemnation unless award is used for replacement
- Gain on obligations purchased for less than face value
- Gain on partner's sale of asset to partnership
- Gain on swap-fund transfers
- Government employees receipt of additional compensation for foreign service employment
- Group legal services
- Illegal transactions that produce money (gambling, illegal businesses, insider's profits, embezzlement, protection money, etc.)
- Illness or sick pay by employer
- Imputed interest on interest-free loans
- Insurance proceeds for business interruption insurance
- Insurance proceeds for loss of profits, use or occupancy
- Layoff pay benefits
- Living quarters and meals not furnished for employer's convenience
- Mortgage indebtedness discount for prepayment
- Non-employee compensation, including payments to independent contractors
- Notary public fees received
- Partnership distributive share of taxable income
- Punitive damages

- Receiver's fees
- Rewards—such as crimestopper, lost animal, employee suggestion and other awards
- Security deposits retained by lessor
- Taxes for employee that are paid by employer
- Taxes paid by lessee for benefit of lessor
- Tenancy surrender payments
- Trust and estate distributions that represent income, not principal
- Tuition paid by employer unless under qualified plans
- Vacation fund allowance under union agreement

APPENDIX B

SOURCES OF NON-TAXABLE INCOME

- Accident and health insurance reimbursements, unless you claimed a deduction for the medical expenses when paid
- Allowances received by dependents of deceased military personnel
- Athletic facilities use on employer's premises
- Bad debt recovery, if no prior deduction was claimed
- Bequests
- Business interruption insurance proceeds based on per day idleness
- Business subsidies for construction or capital contributions
- Capital contributions to corporation
- Combat zone pay
- Damages for personal injuries or sickness
- Damages for slander or libel of personal reputation
- Death benefits paid by employer, up to $5,000
- Dependent care assistance program payments
- Employee discounts
- Endowment policy proceeds, until cost recovered
- Fringe benefits, if due to working conditions or *de minimis* value
- Gain on sale of personal residence, if qualified replacement purchased or $125,000 if qualified and over 55
- Gifts
- Income tax refunds, federal
- Inheritances
- Interest on veterans' life insurance dividends converted to additional coverage

- Interest on wrap-around annuity contracts sold by life insurance companies
- Involuntary conversion gains that are reinvested
- Life insurance group-term premiums paid by employer for $50,000 or less of insurance
- Life insurance proceeds paid on death of the insured
- Living expenses while damaged home is being repaired
- Medical care payments from employer-financed accident and health plan
- Moving expenses reimbursed by employer
- Mustering-out pay (when you are paid to leave the military)
- National Service Life Insurance dividends
- Parsonage rental value furnished to minister or rabbi, including rental allowances
- Peace Corps volunteers' basic living and travel allowances
- Pensions or annuities for personal injuries or sickness resulting from active military service or in the U.S. Foreign Service, Public Health Service work, or National Oceanic and Atmospheric Administration
- Political campaign contributions, with certain exceptions
- Rebates, credits and price reductions received by customers
- Retirement distributions of previously taxed employee contributions
- Renter's improvements value to lessor upon termination of lease
- Stock options not yet exercised
- Strike benefits to employees in need
- Supper money paid for employer's benefit
- Treaty-exempt income—income earned that is non-taxable under a treaty
- Trust and estate distributions that represent principal, not interest
- Veterans' benefits
- Workers' Compensation payments

INDEX

ESTATE PLANNING & PROBATE

Make Your Own Living Trust, Clifford	1st Ed	$19.95	LITR
Plan Your Estate With a Living Trust, Clifford	2nd Ed	$19.95	NEST
Nolo's Simple Will Book, Clifford	2nd Ed	$17.95	SWIL
Who Will Handle Your Finances If You Can't?, Clifford & Randolph	1st Ed	$19.95	FINA
The Conservatorship Book (California), Goldoftas & Farren	2nd Ed	$29.95	CNSV
How to Probate an Estate (California), Nissley	7th Ed	$34.95	PAE
Nolo's Law Form Kit: Wills, Clifford & Goldoftas	1st Ed	$14.95	KWL
Write Your Will (audio cassette), Warner & Greene	1st Ed	$14.95	TWYW
5 Ways to Avoid Probate (audio cassette), Warner & Greene	1st Ed	$14.95	TPRO

GOING TO COURT

Represent Yourself in Court, Bergman & Berman-Barrett	1st Ed	$29.95	RYC
Everybody's Guide to Municipal Court (California), Duncan	1st Ed	$29.95	MUNI
Everybody's Guide to Small Claims Court (California), Warner	11th Ed	$18.95	CSCC
Everybody's Guide to Small Claims Court (National), Warner	5th Ed	$18.95	NSCC
Fight Your Ticket (California), Brown	5th Ed	$18.95	FYT
Collect Your Court Judgment (California), Scott, Elias & Goldoftas	2nd Ed	$19.95	JUDG
How to Change Your Name (California), Loeb & Brown	6th Ed	$24.95	NAME
The Criminal Records Book (California), Siegel	3rd Ed	$19.95	CRIM
Winning in Small Claims Court, Warner & Greene (audio cassette)	1st Ed	$14.95	TWIN

LEGAL REFORM

Fed Up with the Legal System, Nolo Press	2nd Ed	$9.95	LEG

= BOOKS WITH DISK

TO ORDER CALL 800-992-6656

BUSINESS & WORKPLACE

💾 Software Development: A Legal Guide, Fishman	1st Ed	$44.95	SFT
The Legal Guide for Starting & Running a Small Business, Steingold	1st Ed	$22.95	RUNS
Sexual Harassment on the Job, Petrocelli & Repa	1st Ed	$14.95	HARS
Your Rights in the Workplace, Repa	2nd Ed	$15.95	YRW
How to Write a Business Plan, McKeever	4th Ed	$19.95	SBS
Marketing Without Advertising, Phillips & Rasberry	1st Ed	$14.00	MWAD
The Partnership Book, Clifford & Warner	4th Ed	$24.95	PART`
The California Nonprofit Corporation Handbook, Mancuso	6th Ed	$29.95	NON
💾 The California Nonprofit Corporation Handbook, Mancuso	DOS	$39.95	NPI
	MAC	$39.95	NPM
💾 How to Form a Nonprofit Corporation (National), Mancuso	DOS	$39.95	NNP
How to Form Your Own California Corporation, Mancuso	7th Ed	$29.95	CCOR
How to Form Your Own California Corporation with Corporate Records Binder and Disk, Mancuso	1st Ed	$39.95	CACI
The California Professional Corporation Handbook, Mancuso	5th Ed	$34.95	PROF
💾 How to Form Your Own Florida Corporation, Mancuso	DOS	$39.95	FLCO
How to Form Your Own New York Corporation, Mancuso	2nd Ed	$29.95	NYCO
💾 How to Form Your Own New York Corporation, Mancuso	DOS	$39.95	NYCI
How to Form Your Own Texas Corporation, Mancuso	4th Ed	$29.95	TCOR
💾 How to Form Your Own Texas Corporation, Mancuso	DOS	$39.95	TCI
The Independent Paralegal's Handbook, Warner	2nd Ed	$24.95	PARA
Getting Started as an Independent Paralegal, Warner (audio cassette)	2nd Ed	$44.95	GSIP
How To Start Your Own Business: Small Business Law, Warner & Greene (audio cassette)	1st Ed	$14.95	TBUS

THE NEIGHBORHOOD

Neighbor Law: Fences, Trees, Boundaries & Noise, Jordan	1st Ed	$14.95	NEI
Safe Home, Safe Neighborhoods: Stopping Crime Where You Live, Mann & Blakeman	1st Ed	$14.95	SAFE
Dog Law, Randolph	2nd Ed	$12.95	DOG

MONEY MATTERS

Stand Up to the IRS, Daily	2nd Ed	$21.95	SIRS
Money Troubles: Legal Strategies to Cope With Your Debts, Leonard	2nd Ed	$16.95	MT
How to File for Bankruptcy, Elias, Renauer & Leonard	4th Ed	$25.95	HFB

💾 **= BOOKS WITH DISK**

Simple Contracts for Personal Use, Elias & Stewart	2nd Ed	$16.95	CONT
Nolo's Law Form Kit: Power of Attorney,Clifford, Randolph & Goldoftas	1st Ed	$14.95	KPA
Nolo's Law Form Kit: Personal Bankruptcy, Elias, Renauer, Leonard & Goldoftas	1st Ed	$14.95	KBNK
Nolo's Law Form Kit: Rebuild Your Credit, Leonard & Goldoftas	1st Ed	$14.95	KCRD
Nolo's Law Form Kit: Loan Agreements, Stewart & Goldoftas	1st Ed	$14.95	KLOAN
Nolo's Law Form Kit: Buy & Sell Contracts, Elias, Stewart & Goldoftas	1st Ed	$9.95	KCONT

FAMILY MATTERS

How to Raise or Lower Child Support In California, Duncan & Siegal	2nd Ed	$17.95	CHLD
Divorce & Money, Woodhouse & Felton-Collins with Blakeman	2nd Ed	$21.95	DIMO
The Living Together Kit, Ihara & Warner	6th Ed	$17.95	LTK
The Guardianship Book (California), Goldoftas & Brown	1st Ed	$19.95	GB
A Legal Guide for Lesbian and Gay Couples, Curry & Clifford	8th Ed	$24.95	LG
How to Do Your Own Divorce in California, Sherman	19th Ed	$21.95	CDIV
Practical Divorce Solutions, Sherman	1st Ed	$14.95	PDS
California Marriage & Divorce Law, Warner, Ihara & Elias	11th Ed	$19.95	MARR
How to Adopt Your Stepchild in California, Zagone & Randolph	4th Ed	$22.95	ADOP
Nolo's Pocket Guide to Family Law, Leonard & Elias	3rd Ed	$14.95	FLD
Divorce: A New Yorker's Guide to Doing it Yourself, *Alexandra*	1st Ed	$24.95	NYDIV

JUST FOR FUN

29 Reasons Not to Go to Law School, Warner & Ihara	3rd Ed	$9.95	29R
Devil's Advocates, Roth & Roth	1st Ed	$12.95	DA
Poetic Justice, Roth & Roth	1st Ed	$9.95	PJ

PATENT, COPYRIGHT & TRADEMARK

Trademark: How To Name Your Business & Product, McGrath & Elias, with Shena	1st Ed	$29.95	TRD
Patent It Yourself, Pressman	3rd Ed	$39.95	PAT
The Inventor's Notebook, Grissom & Pressman	1st Ed	$19.95	INOT
The Copyright Handbook, Fishman	2nd Ed	$24.95	COHA

LANDLORDS & TENANTS

The Landlord's Law Book, Vol. 1: Rights & Responsibilities (California), Brown & Warner	4th Ed	$32.95	LBRT
The Landlord's Law Book, Vol. 2: Evictions (California), Brown	4th Ed	$32.95	LBEV

Tenants' Rights (California), Moskovitz & Warner	11th Ed	$15.95	CTEN
Nolo's Law Form Kit: Leases & Rental Agreements (California), Warner & Stewart	1st Ed	$14.95	KLEAS

HOMEOWNERS

How to Buy a House in California, Warner, Serkes & Devine	3rd Ed	$24.95	BHCA
For Sale By Owner, Devine	2nd Ed	$24.95	FSBO
Homestead Your House, Warner, Sherman & Ihara	8th Ed	$9.95	HOME
The Deeds Book, Randolph	2nd Ed	$15.95	DEED

OLDER AMERICANS

Beat the Nursing Home Trap: A Consumer's Guide to Choosing & Financing Long Term Care, Matthews	2nd Ed	$18.95	ELD
Social Security, Medicare & Pensions, Matthews with Berman	5th Ed	$18.95	SOA

RESEARCH/REFERENCE

Legal Research, Elias & Levinkind	3rd Ed	$19.95	LRES
Legal Research Made Easy: A Roadmap Through the Law Library Maze (2 1/2 hr videotape & manual), Nolo & Legal Star	1st Ed	$89.95	LRME

CONSUMER

How to Get A Green Card: Legal Ways To Stay In The U.S.A., Lewis with Madlanscay	1st Ed	$22.95	GRN
How to Win Your Personal Injury Claim, Matthews	1st Ed	$24.95	PICL
Nolo's Pocket Guide to California Law, Guerin & Nolo Press Editors	2nd Ed	$10.95	CLAW
Nolo's Pocket Guide to California Law on Disk	Windows	$24.95	CLWIN
	MAC	$24.95	CLM
Nolo's Law Form Kit: Hiring Child Care & Household Help, Repa & Goldoftas	1st Ed	$14.95	KCHLD
Nolo's Pocket Guide to Consumer Rights, Kaufman	2nd Ed	$12.95	CAG

IMMIGRATION

How to Get a Green Card: Legal Ways to Stay in the U.S.A., Lewis with Madlanscay	1st Ed	$22.95	GRN

TO ORDER CALL 800-992-6656

SOFTWARE

WillMaker 5.0	Windows	$69.95	WI5
	DOS	$69.95	WI5
	MAC	$69.95	WM5
Nolo's Personal RecordKeeper 3.0	DOS	$49.95	FRI3
	MAC	$49.95	FRM3
Nolo's Living Trust 1.0	MAC	$79.95	LTM1
Nolo's Partnership Maker 1.0	DOS	$129.95	PAGI1
California Incorporator 1.0	DOS	$129.00	INCI
Patent It Yourself 1.0	Windows	$229.95	PYW1

RECYCLE YOUR OUT-OF-DATE BOOKS AND GET 25% OFF YOUR NEXT PURCHASE

It's important to have the most current legal information. Because laws and legal procedures change often, we update our books regularly. To help keep you up-to-date we are extending this special offer. Cut out and mail the title portion of the cover of any old Nolo book with your next order and we'll give you a 25% discount off the retail price of ANY new Nolo book you purchase directly from us. For current prices and editions call us at 1 (800) 992-6656.

This offer is to individuals only. Prices subject to change.

VISIT OUR STORE

If you live in the Bay Area, be sure to visit the Nolo Press Bookstore on the corner of 9th & Parker Streets in west Berkeley. You'll find our complete line of books and software—all at a discount. CALL 1-510-704-2248 for hours.

TO ORDER CALL 800-992-6656

ORDER FORM

Code	Quantity	Title	Unit price	Total

Subtotal	
California residents add Sales Tax	
Shipping & Handling ($4 for 1st item; $1 each additional)	
2nd day UPS (additional $5; $8 in Alaska and Hawaii)	
TOTAL	

Name

Address

(UPS to street address, Priority Mail to P.O. boxes)

FOR FASTER SERVICE, USE YOUR CREDIT CARD AND OUR TOLL-FREE NUMBERS

Monday-Friday, 7 a.m. to 6 p.m. Pacific Time

Order Line   1 (800) 992-6656 (in the 510 area code, call 549-1976)
General Information 1 (510) 549-1976
Fax your order   1 (800) 645-0895 (in the 510 area code, call 548-5902)

METHOD OF PAYMENT

☐ Check enclosed
☐ VISA   ☐ Mastercard   ☐ Discover Card   ☐ American Express

Account #   Expiration Date

Authorizing Signature

Daytime Phone

Allow 2-3 weeks for delivery. Prices subject to change.

NOLO PRESS, 950 PARKER ST., BERKELEY, CA 94710

SAVMO

TO ORDER CALL 800-992-6656

When you register, we'll send you our quarterly newspaper, the *Nolo News*, free for two years. (U.S. addresses only.) Here's what you'll get in every issue:

■ INFORMATIVE ARTICLES

Written by Nolo editors, articles provide practical legal information on issues you encounter in everyday life: family law, wills, debts, consumer rights, and much more.

■ UPDATE SERVICE

The *Nolo News* keeps you informed of legal changes that affect any Nolo book and software program.

■ BOOK AND SOFTWARE REVIEWS

We're always looking for good legal and consumer books and software from other publishers. When we find them, we review them and offer them in our mail order catalog.

■ ANSWERS TO YOUR LEGAL QUESTIONS

Our readers are always challenging us with good questions on a variety of legal issues. So in each issue, "Auntie Nolo" gives sage advice and sound information.

■ COMPLETE NOLO PRESS CATALOG

The *Nolo News* contains an up-to-the-minute catalog of all Nolo books and software, which you can order using our "800" toll-free order line. And you can see at a glance if you're using an out-of-date version of a Nolo product.

■ LAWYER JOKES

Nolo's famous lawyer joke column continually gets the goat of the legal establishment. If we print a joke you send in, you'll get a $20 Nolo gift certificate.

We promise *never* to give your name and address to any other organization.

COMPLETE AND MAIL TODAY

SMART WAYS TO SAVE MONEY DURING AND AFTER DIVORCE   Registration Card

We'd like to know what you think! Please take a moment to fill out and return this postage paid card for a free two year subscription to the *Nolo News*. If you already receive the *Nolo News*, we'll extend your subscription.

Name _____ Ph.(   ) _____

Address _____

City _____ State _____ Zip _____

Where did you hear about this book? _____

For what purpose did you use this book? _____

Did you consult a lawyer?	Yes	No		Not Applicable			
Was it easy for you to use this book?	(very easy)	5	4	3	2	1	(very difficult)
Did you find this book helpful?	(very)	5	4	3	2	1	(not at all)

Comments _____

_____

_____

_____

_____

THANK YOU   **SAVMO 1.0**

[Nolo books are]..."written in plain language, free of legal mumbo jumbo, and spiced with witty personal observations."

—ASSOCIATED PRESS

"Well-produced and slickly written, the [Nolo] books are designed to take the mystery out of seemingly involved procedures, carefully avoiding legalese and leading the reader step-by-step through such everyday legal problems as filling out forms, making up contracts, and even how to behave in court."

—SAN FRANCISCO EXAMINER

"...Nolo publications...guide people simply through the how, when, where and why of law."

—WASHINGTON POST

"Increasingly, people who are not lawyers are performing tasks usually regarded as legal work... And consumers, using books like Nolo's, do routine legal work themselves."

—NEW YORK TIMES

"...All of [Nolo's] books are easy-to-understand, are updated regularly, provide pull-out forms...and are often quite moving in their sense of compassion for the struggles of the lay reader."

—SAN FRANCISCO CHRONICLE